POLYVAGAL THEORY IN THE CLASSROOM

Polyvagal Theory provides a breakdown of how the nervous system responds and reacts to unconscious messages of safety and threat. This accessible guide explores Polyvagal Theory and its potential for fully understanding and supporting the behaviours of children and young people in emotional distress at school.

By exploring how early childhood experiences – such as abuse, trauma, an insecure attachment, or bereavement – can have a detrimental impact on the development of the child's nervous system, we can view their behaviours in a new light.

Polyvagal Theory in the Classroom:

- Contains a wealth of activities to use in the classroom
- Delves into new understandings of what is happening to children and young people when they become dysregulated
- Introduces practical ways to support pupils' emotional wellbeing, promote better mental health, and help to develop their capacity to self-regulate
- Contains practice exercises which provide opportunities for the reader to reflect on their own practice.

Packed full of case studies to bring theory to life, this book builds skills to gain awareness and control of our own nervous systems and to become the safe and calm presence for the overwhelmed child. This empowering book is essential reading for mainstream primary and secondary teachers, SENCOs and teaching support staff.

Sarah Butler is a child and adolescent therapist, offering bespoke guidance on therapeutic approaches to managing the behaviours of children who have experienced trauma, bereavement, abuse and/or insecure attachments. Sarah is also an experienced teacher, having worked in mainstream secondary schools and alternative provisions, including more than a decade teaching in a hospital school within an adolescent psychiatric unit, where she developed and delivered mental health awareness training to local schools and trainee teachers.

POLYVAGAL THEORY IN THE CLASSROOM

A Guide to Empower Educators and Support Dysregulated Children and Young People

Sarah Butler

Routledge
Taylor & Francis Group

LONDON AND NEW YORK

Cover image: Getty/Moncherie

First published 2024
by Routledge
4 Park Square, Milton Park, Abingdon, Oxon OX14 4RN

and by Routledge
605 Third Avenue, New York, NY 10158

Routledge is an imprint of the Taylor & Francis Group, an informa business

© 2024 Sarah Butler

British Library Cataloguing-in-Publication Data
A catalogue record for this book is available from the British Library

ISBN: 978-1-032-50029-4 (hbk)
ISBN: 978-1-032-50027-0 (pbk)
ISBN: 978-1-003-39657-4 (ebk)

DOI: 10.4324/9781003396574

Typeset in Interstate
by SPi Technologies India Pvt Ltd (Straive)

This book is dedicated to all the young people who lost their battle with mental illness, and tragically took their own lives.

CONTENTS

ACKNOWLEDGEMENTS

I would like to thank friends and family for their unwavering support with this endeavour, in particular, Steph Yates who offered the benefit of her experience and wisdom from the very beginning and throughout.

And a big thank you to all the children and young people I have had the pleasure of working with, who have let me into their worlds and taught me so much.

Introduction

> It was the start of the lesson and I could see the girl who had just sat down in the front was upset. The other pupils were still slowly arriving, so I had a few minutes. I sat next to her and spoke gently, asking what had happened and what might help. She looked at me, but was then distracted by a boy sitting across the table who wasn't happy with how I was dealing with the situation. He called across with demands to let her leave the classroom. I turned back to the girl, who was quietly trying to tell me something. I missed what she was saying due to the shouts from the boy. He was becoming angry. The girl was now crying and starting to shake. I asked him to stop shouting. He stood up, glaring at me, shouting louder. I could feel my heart starting to pound. I put down the piece of paper I had been holding as I could see it was shaking in my hands. I needed to regain control but I couldn't think clearly.

As a teacher, or other education professional, you may well have similar stories of challenging incidents in your place of work. Moments where you were pushed to the limits of your capacity to regulate your own emotional state. Moments that stayed with you and followed you home at the end of the day.

Teaching staff are in the position of caring for the emotional worlds of children and young people, while trying to manage their own emotional wellbeing, and at times, this is a real challenge. Stress levels are notoriously high in the teaching profession, and for some time there has been the problem of more teachers leaving the profession than entering it, resulting in ongoing teacher shortages throughout the UK.

I spent a decade in mainstream secondary, teaching GCSE Science, and I remember all too well the stresses of mainstream teaching, counteracted by that great feeling that I was making a difference in the lives of my pupils. It was teaching the 'hard-to-reach' pupils that I found most rewarding, so I then spent about 15 years teaching in alternative education settings, including a Pupil Referral Unit, and a hospital school within an adolescent psychiatric unit. I finally left teaching once I had trained as a Play and Creative Arts Therapist, and I now have a therapy practice working 1:1 with children and young people aged 4-16. It was during my training that I came across this new theory that uses the science of how the mind and

DOI: 10.4324/9781003396574-1

body work together, to give a new understanding to emotional states. I found it fascinating. The scientist in me enthused at the idea of linking human physiology to emotional wellbeing. I started applying the theory in my therapy sessions and soon realised that it was applicable in my teaching at the psychiatric unit. I eagerly told my teaching colleagues about the theory and how to apply it to our interactions with the young people. I was then asked to give a talk about it at a conference, 'Units United', for teachers from similar units throughout the UK. The response at the conference was overwhelmingly positive, and I came to realise this was a theory that *all* teachers, in *all* educational settings, should be told about. I also found I had so much more to say than I could fit into an hour-long talk – I had enough to write a book!

Once I had decided to write this book, I felt a sense of urgency, like I was privy to some new vital information that I needed to tell every teacher about. It seems that not a day goes by without a news report on the state of the next generation's mental health. Mental health difficulties in young people and children are on the rise and becoming a serious concern, especially since the global pandemic, which raised anxieties throughout the world. One review of research evidence found *significant* impacts of the 2020 school closures on anxiety and depressive symptoms in children and young people and increased suicide rates, along with evidence suggesting unmet mental health needs (Viner et al., 2022). As I write this, three years on from the pandemic, I am seeing a noticeable increase in the number of children and young people referred to me for therapeutic support due to *new* difficulties relating to anxiety. Other child and adolescent therapists I have spoken to have found the same.

Some of the first professionals to notice the emerging mental health issues in children and young people are education staff. With limited mental health services to support the growing need, school staff are often left trying to manage challenging behaviours driven by emotional distress, with little training, guidance or support from outside agencies.

Polyvagal Theory is a new science-based approach to understanding the behaviours of people in emotional distress in terms of their physiology. It has been widely adopted by eminent trauma specialists and has been cited in more than 10,000 peer-reviewed articles by specialists from various disciplines. In an education setting, the understanding of Polyvagal Theory can be applied to support a pupil with challenging behaviours, reducing emerging mental health illnesses, and developing the emotional wellbeing of children, young people *and* the professionals themselves. In this book we will explore child development and the impacts of childhood trauma through the lens of Polyvagal Theory. We will examine the causes of the challenging behaviours we see in pupils, look at new ways to think about these behaviours as reactions to unconscious drives, adopting an attitude of *honouring* the behaviour that has been helping the young person survive, and develop new skills for supporting dysregulated pupils.

The Structure of the Book

This book is organised into two parts, where Part I focuses on the *understanding* of Polyvagal Theory and Part II on the *application* of the theory in the school setting.

Part I covers the basics of Polyvagal Theory, and how we can use it to understand child development, early childhood trauma and the behaviours of pupils in school. This section of the book also explores how you can use your understanding of Polyvagal Theory to help improve your own emotional wellbeing as well as that of your pupils.

Part II gives over 50 classroom activities covering the age range 4–18 years, for use with whole classes or groups of pupils, to give them an age-appropriate understanding of Polyvagal Theory and exercises, using this understanding to improve their emotional wellbeing. There are also more than 20 exercises for 1:1 work with the pupils who need extra support.

At the end of each chapter and the end of Part II, you will find bullet point summaries of learning points, for quick reminders should you need to dip back into the book after reading it through. There are also practical exercises at the end of many chapters and often throughout, to practise the application of the theoretical learning. At the end of the book, you will find a Glossary of terms used to support your understanding of Polyvagal Theory and the other ideas covered in this book. The terms are given in bold in the text on their first occurrence in the chapter.

In some chapters there are references to a child's caregivers, especially in the discussions on child development and childhood trauma. For better readability I have opted to use the term 'mother' for the primary caregiver, but this is intended to include anyone in the role of primary caregiver, such as the father, grandparent, foster carer, etc. Where I have referred to a child's 'parents', this should be read to include any caregivers in the role of parents, such as adoptive parents, step-parents, etc. My thinking here is that you don't have to be a biological mother or parent in order to mother or parent a child.

Your own understanding of Polyvagal Theory is essential to the efficacy of the practical activities in Part II, so I strongly recommend taking your time to fully digest the insights in Part I. Investing your time and energy in the exercises throughout Part I should provide you with a transformative experience, which will not only influence your approach to working with your pupils, but also will open up a new understanding of yourself.

PART I

Understanding Polyvagal Theory

1 What Is Polyvagal Theory?

In this chapter, we will be exploring various aspects of **Polyvagal Theory**, starting with an overview of the central nervous system, and introducing the autonomic nervous system. A basic overview of the evolution of the brain will be followed by an explanation of the three **autonomic states**, demonstrated through scenarios and anecdotes. At the end of the chapter, you will find a summary of the learning points and a practical exercise to try. For now, we will focus on a general understanding of Polyvagal Theory, but in later chapters we will apply it more directly to the school environment.

Background to Polyvagal Theory

It was in 1994 that Stephen Porges, a distinguished professor of psychiatry and university scientist, first proposed Polyvagal Theory. The theory was further developed and in recent years has been adopted by prominent traumatologists, such as Bessel Van Der Kolk, Peter Levine and Pat Ogden, leading to innovative treatments in **trauma** therapy. Polyvagal Theory gives us an understanding of how our **autonomic nervous system** (ANS) reacts to ordinary and extraordinary experiences. The theory links the evolution of the mammalian autonomic nervous system to social behaviour.

Stephen Porges refers to Polyvagal Theory as 'the science of safety', so we will need to start with a brief overview of the actual science: a biology lesson on the central nervous system. Rest assured, I will try to make this easy to follow and keep the technical jargon to a minimum. To help with the understanding of the concepts, there is a Glossary of terms at the back of the book, including some extra terms not mentioned in the book, in case you decide to read further on the subject.

The Central Nervous System

Your **central nervous system** is made up of three main parts: your brain, your spinal column, and your network of nerves. Its function is to facilitate two-way communication between your brain and your body. As you'll be aware, there are nerves throughout your body sending signals to your brain (via the spinal column) from your senses. Right now, as you read this book,

DOI: 10.4324/9781003396574-3

your eyes will be sending signals through your optic nerve to your brain. Nerves connected to the skin all over your body will be telling you whether you are hot, cold or comfortable. Signals will be coming from your ears, tongue and nose, telling your brain what you can hear, taste and smell. But there are also nerves connected internally to your organs, telling you whether you need the toilet, whether you're hungry, and sending information about any aches or pains within your body, etc. Your brain is also sending signals back along nerves to your body in response to this information. For instance, your brain may tell your body to sweat more to cool you down if you're hot, or it may cause you to look in the direction of an unexpected sound you just heard.

The Autonomic Nervous System

Interestingly, out of all the information travelling back and forth through your central nervous system, you will only be consciously aware of less than 1 per cent of it (Dispenza, 2007). The rest happens below your level of awareness, in other words *unconsciously*. This unconscious activity happens in a part of the central nervous system known as the autonomic nervous system (ANS). The whole purpose of your ANS is to ensure your survival. Your ANS is currently monitoring and controlling your heartrate and breathing, controlling your digestion, regulating your hormones and metabolism and maintaining numerous other processes needed for your body to live (see Figure 1.1).

Your ANS has another very important role related to your survival. It continually scans your environment and your body for signs of threat and signs of safety. If it detects any signs of threat, it quickly responds without any involvement of your conscious mind. In other words, your ANS will cause changes in your body and in your behaviour when it detects threat, and you will have no conscious control over these responses. As you are focused on reading this book, if you suddenly heard a loud bang very nearby, your ANS is likely to make your body 'jump'. Your muscles are likely to tense up and you would turn towards the source

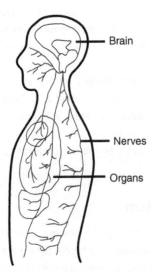

Brain

Nerves

Organs

Figure 1.1 The human body showing nerves of the autonomic nervous system connecting various parts of the body to the brain

of the noise, with your eyes wide until you have assessed whether there is actually a danger. You wouldn't *consciously* think about these body reactions, they happen automatically under the control of your ANS. Your conscious thinking mind becomes involved *after* the automatic ANS responses. Similarly, if you feel a sudden sharp pain in your side, your ANS may cause you to wince and clutch your side, as you bend in an attempt to relieve the pain. Again, there is no *conscious* thinking process involved in your body's response. You don't *decide* to wince, to clutch your side, to jump at a loud noise. The responses and actions caused by your ANS are *unconscious*; they are *below* your level of awareness and control.

The Evolution of the Brain

Long ago, when humans were living in a world where they had natural predators sharing their habitat, their survival relied heavily upon speedy responses to threat. The ANS is connected at the top of the spinal cord to the most ancient part of the human brain – the **brainstem** (also known as the **'reptilian' brain**, as we share this brain structure with reptiles). All information from the body passes through the brainstem before it is processed by the relevant parts of the brain. This processing takes time, so when there is an immediate threat, the ANS and brainstem take action before the rest of the brain becomes involved.

Just above the brainstem is the **limbic system** (or the **mammalian brain**, common to all mammals) which is predominantly associated with emotions, social behaviour and attachment.

Then the third layer of the human brain is the newest part in our evolution, the **neocortex**, which is our thinking brain. The neocortex is where language, learning, problem-solving, understanding sensory information and all other higher brain functions happen. Right now, your neocortex is making sense of these words and picturing the different parts of the brain to form a new understanding.

Of course, the brain is far more complex but this simple three-part model, known as the **triune brain** (Figure 1.2) is all we need for our understanding of Polyvagal Theory.

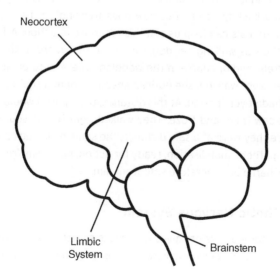

Figure 1.2 The triune brain showing the brainstem, limbic system and neocortex

The ANS has two parts which can be thought of like the accelerator and brake pedals in a car: The **sympathetic nervous system** (the accelerator) and the **parasympathetic nervous system** (the brake).

The Sympathetic Nervous System

The sympathetic nervous system puts us in a mobilised state, giving us the 'fight, flight or freeze' response, which you may have heard of. When your sympathetic nervous system takes control in response to a possible threat detected by your ANS, your body gets ready for action.

In the sympathetic mobilisation state:

- Your heartrate increases.
- You breathe faster.
- Blood rushes to your limbs so you are ready to run, fight or freeze.
- Your pupils dilate (to allow more light in).
- Your digestion slows as the blood supply to your internal organs decreases (this could give sensations such as 'butterflies' or stomach-ache).
- You cannot think clearly or communicate well.

If your sympathetic nervous system was completely in control of your body right now, you would not be able to understand what you are reading at all, as your neocortex (thinking brain) would be offline. Your body would be in survival mode. Another process which happens in the neocortex is our experience of empathy, so when taken over by sympathetic mobilisation, you would not be able to empathise with another person. The sympathetic nervous system does, however, involve the limbic system part of the brain, so your own intense emotions could be felt, such as anxiety, panic, fear, terror or rage.

At this point, it may be worth exploring the 'freeze' response to threat. It would make sense that if you feel under threat, running away (flight) or defending yourself physically (fight) could bring you back to safety. But how does freezing on the spot help deal with a threat? The world of animals can help us see this response in action. A friend once told me about a time when she was walking her dog, Charlie, in the woods. Like many dogs, Charlie loved to chase squirrels, and of course in the woodland there were plenty of squirrels scurrying around. As they were walking, she noticed ahead of them a squirrel very close to their path, which Charlie hadn't yet spotted. At this distance, the squirrel would not have been able to outrun Charlie. It saw them and froze. They walked right by the squirrel without Charlie noticing it at all. Once they were at a safe distance, the squirrel darted up a tree. The squirrel was in a state of sympathetic mobilisation, ready for action, but it was *freezing* that made the squirrel invisible to Charlie and therefore safe from him.

The Parasympathetic Nervous System

The parasympathetic nervous system gives us what is sometimes referred to as a 'rest and digest' state, and slows things down. Heartrate drops, breathing slows and there is reduced tension in the body. This system is active when you are relaxing at the end of the day in front of a good film or meeting up with friends for a coffee and catch-up. Take a moment before you read further to notice how fast your heart is beating, how fast you are breathing and whether you feel any muscle tension in your body. If everything feels slow, steady, and relaxed, then your parasympathetic nervous system is currently active.

For a long time, it was thought that the parasympathetic nervous system was only associated with a state of calm, relaxation and safety. Polyvagal Theory gives us another role for the parasympathetic nervous system, due to the two parts of the nerve responsible: the **vagus nerve** (Porges, 2017).

The Vagus Nerve

The nerve connecting your brainstem to your body in the parasympathetic nervous system is called the vagus nerve. Its name comes from the Latin for 'wanderer' as it is such a long nerve, starting in the brain and wandering down the neck towards the heart, lungs and then the rest of the internal organs. It also has strong connections in the face and contributes to facial expressions.

The vagus nerve splits into two parts: the **ventral vagal nerve** and the **dorsal vagal nerve**.

The Ventral Vagal Nerve

It is the ventral vagal nerve that gives us the sense of calm, safety and connectedness with others. Hopefully, you have your ventral vagal nerve online as you are reading, because it allows your neocortex to function efficiently, and you are therefore able to think about what you are reading and make sense of it.

The main role of the ventral vagal nerve is to regulate the heartrate and breathing, but interestingly it uses social engagement to do this. There is a strong connection between the face and the heart via the ventral vagal nerve (Porges, 2009). When we talk with others, our facial expressions contribute significantly to our communication. So, when you receive non-verbal signals of safety from another person, such as a warm smile, your social engagement system is activated, and your **ventral vagal state** is strengthened.

In the ventral vagal state:

- Your heartrate and breathing are steady and vary according to your activity.
- Functions in your body, such as digestion, are at their most efficient.
- Hormone levels and metabolism are under control.
- You are able to think clearly and connect with other people.

When in this state, not only can we communicate and connect with others effectively, but we can also experience **empathy**. These are all functions of the neocortex which operates at its most efficient when in the ventral vagal state. In this state, we are at our best when it comes to understanding our own emotions and the emotions of others. Let's look at an example of the ventral vagal state in action:

It's Saturday morning at the start of the summer half-term break and Kate is preparing breakfast for her two children, ready for a day at the park with friends. She is quietly humming to the radio, as she puts the kettle on, and planning what food to pack for their picnic. Then she notices her youngest, Lucy, standing in the doorway staring mournfully at the floor. Kate stops what she is doing and asks, 'What's wrong, sweetie?' No answer. Kate walks over to Lucy, squats down to bring herself to Lucy's level and takes hold of Lucy's hands. 'You look sad, Lucy, tell me what's wrong.' Lucy looks at her mum and starts explaining that she doesn't want to meet their friends at the park because she was afraid of their dog. Kate puts her arms around Lucy and reassures her. Together they make a plan to help Lucy feel safe about meeting their friends at the park.

Through the Polyvagal Lens ...

We can tell that Kate is in her ventral vagal state, by her relaxed humming to the radio and her clear thinking while preparing breakfast and planning the day. When she sees her daughter, she experiences empathy as she quickly understands that Lucy is unhappy. Kate responds empathically as she notices Lucy's feelings aloud. She communicates her care and concern both verbally and through her body language. Kate's empathy, effective communication and planning are all happening in her neocortex, which can only operate this well because Kate is in her ventral vagal state.

The Dorsal Vagal Nerve

Polyvagal Theory tells us there is a second line of defence, for situations where sympathetic mobilisation cannot deal with the threat. This is where the dorsal vagal nerve comes into action and shuts the body down (Porges, 2017).

In the animal kingdom, we see this where prey feign death when they have been caught by a predator. This could give the message to the predator that their prey was already dead, so is not a 'fresh kill' and therefore may not be safe to eat. The predator may discard the prey. At this point, the prey's sympathetic nervous system activates, and they can run away and hide. The dorsal shutdown can be seen as a survival strategy. This is a very different response to the sympathetic mobilisation state of 'freeze', with which it can easily be confused. In order to fool the predator into thinking their prey is dead, the body of the prey would become floppy and lifeless. In contrast, the sympathetic mobilisation state of 'freeze' causes the body to become tense, rigid and ready for action.

There is, however, another side to the state of dorsal shutdown. It can be viewed as *preparation* for death. In cases of trauma, especially if survival is threatened, the dorsal vagal state can take over. Pain receptors can be dampened in this state, to protect the brain from experiencing the physical pain of the trauma. There can be a **dissociation**, where the mind disconnects from the body, thereby limiting the psychological effects of the trauma.

In a complete dorsal shutdown state:

- Your breathing slows significantly and becomes shallow.
- Year heartrate slows.
- Digestion and all functions of the internal organs stop (which can lead to the bladder and bowels emptying).
- Almost all movement is disabled, so the body is in a state of collapse.
- You would be unable to speak or understand words spoken to you.
- You would lose connection to your senses.
- You might faint.

In this state, the neocortex is disabled, which means the social engagement system is offline, memories are not formed properly, and no sense can be made of what is happening. Activity of the limbic system is limited so emotions may seem switched off. With the neocortex unable to process the experience, the memory of the trauma may become 'stuck' within the limbic system and cause symptoms such as flashbacks and nightmares in the traumatised person, long after the trauma is over.

The Three Autonomic States

So far, I have given you an overview of the three **autonomic states**, with descriptions of what happens in the body when one of the states is in control:

1. We have the ventral vagal state, which is when we feel safe and connected.
2. We have the first line of defence against threat, the 'fight, flight or freeze' response of sympathetic mobilisation.
3. Finally, we have dorsal shutdown, when sympathetic mobilisation cannot bring us safety and the body starts to shut down.

Polyvagal Theory tells us that when we move between these states, it is always in this order (Porges, 2003). So, for instance, to move from dorsal shutdown to ventral vagal, you would have to move through sympathetic mobilisation, even if only momentarily.

Due to the structure of the ventral vagal nerve (it has a myelinated sheath), signals can move along it relatively fast, meaning connections with others and with your own body are easily made. However, the structure of the dorsal vagal nerve is slightly different (it is unmyelinated) causing signals to travel slower. This means when someone is in dorsal shutdown, it is much harder for them to come out of that state.

Blended States (Dual Activation)

We have looked at some extreme examples of sympathetic mobilisation and dorsal shutdown when these states dominate, but in everyday life this is rarely how we experience our autonomic states. We are far more likely to experience **blended states**, also called **dual activation**. In these examples, the ventral vagal system is online. The activation of sympathetic mobilisation or dorsal shutdown is experienced primarily as a physiological response, with a limited psychological response. In other words, the body sensations are felt strongly, with the emotional experience less so.

It's one of those mornings where everything seems to be going wrong and you're late for work. You discover the resources you'd prepared yesterday for your first lesson are nowhere to be found, your laptop won't switch on, and then the Head walks in, saying she'd like to bring some visitors into your classroom in 20 minutes to see a lesson in action. Panic sets in! You notice your breathing is fast and you can feel your heart pounding against your chest, as you frantically thump the keys of your laptop. Time is running out – the children are arriving. You take a deep breath, close the laptop, then send a child to ask another teacher if they've seen your missing resources, whilst you quickly devise a 'Plan B' lesson.

Through the Polyvagal Lens ...

Although there are no signs of threat to your life, your sympathetic nervous system has been activated. There are threats to your sense of wellbeing, your sense of confidence as a teacher and your sense of control. There is a threat of humiliation and embarrassment at being watched by strangers and the headteacher, at a time when you are feeling wrong-footed. While sympathetic mobilisation is causing fast breathing and increased heartrate, you are still able to think, which tells us you still have ventral vagal activation. You are able to make a plan of action and to communicate effectively with one of the children. This is an example of blended sympathetic mobilisation and ventral vagal.

Playing a fast and exciting game of Dobble with the family, you can feel the sense of exhilaration as you try to find matches on the cards. You slam down your card, shouting the match far louder than you expected, and laugh excitedly. Your hands are shaking, and your arms and shoulders are tense. You can feel your heart beating fast and you keep holding your breath. You laugh together as cards are slammed onto the table and the shouting gets louder.

Through the Polyvagal Lens ...

This is another example of sympathetic mobilisation and ventral vagal in a blended state, but in this case, there are no signs of threat. Although the sympathetic mobilisation and dorsal shutdown states both activate in response to cues of threat detected by the ANS, they can also be activated via the neocortex. In this frantic card game, the excitement of the game activates sympathetic mobilisation physiological responses. The body reactions, such as fast heartrate, tension in the shoulders, arms and hands, and shouting, are all due to sympathetic mobilisation. However, you can think clearly and share laughter with the group, showing social engagement, i.e., vagal ventral activation. There are no signs of threat so you don't experience the fear or panic associated with sympathetic mobilisation. Playing competitive sports would result in a similar blended state.

At the end of a busy week, you're relaxed on the sofa in your PJs, watching Netflix, after filling up on take-away pizza. Your partner is snuggled up with you and you are enjoying each other's company and the sense of cosiness and calm. You can feel your body sinking into the sofa, your breathing is slow and deep, and you can smell the comforting scent of your partner (mixed with the smell of pizza!). You could easily drift off to sleep.

Through the Polyvagal Lens …

The deep sense of relaxation, coupled with social engagement, indicates a blended state of dorsal shutdown with ventral vagal. Again, there are no signs of threat, but the strong sense of safety, intimacy and calm activates the dorsal vagal nerve to send the body into a deep sense of relaxation. The dorsal shutdown state is experienced as physiological (the body responses) and not psychological.

Think back to the COVID-19 pandemic. For long periods of time, the schools were closed to most pupils, and teachers were delivering lessons online, which was something they had little to no training for or experience in.

Sitting in her empty classroom, Miss Day starts a lesson and watches the screen as her class gradually appear. She does her best to smile and present a calm front to her pupils, who seem to be behaving very differently to when she last saw them in class. Only half of them sign in, of which only a few have their cameras on. She stares blankly for a few minutes, feeling a sense of disconnect from them, then starts talking through the plan for the lesson. Sometimes their screens freeze, or they unexpectedly log off, or wander away. It feels like no-one is listening. Miss Day's talking becomes quieter and slower, and her mind drifts to her journey home when she'll have to queue up outside Tesco, 2 metres from the person in front, in her facemask, waiting to buy much-needed supplies for her elderly neighbour who is scared to open his front door. She wonders how her dad is doing – he tested positive yesterday.

Through the Polyvagal Lens …

There were clear signs of threat during the global pandemic. Threats to our lives and the lives of our loved ones, threats to humanity at large. Nobody escaped the panic, fear and anxieties of the pandemic. Many experienced significant loss, extreme loneliness, and depression. The nervous systems of everyone throughout the world would have been affected. Many would have found the 'fight, flight or freeze' state from sympathetic mobilisation ineffective, and therefore would have experienced dorsal shutdown blended with ventral vagal, as was the case for Miss Day. Her low energy, slow and quiet speech, and inability to focus all suggest dorsal shutdown. The fact that she was able to teach her lesson indicates ventral vagal activation, but poor social engagement limited her ventral vagal state.

We cannot underestimate the impact of the COVID-19 pandemic on our emotional well-being and specifically on our autonomic nervous systems. I believe it would be detrimental to the mental health of our young people for us to consider life as back to normal now the pandemic is coming to an end. The repercussions of the lockdowns, social distancing, closed schools, communicating through facemasks, and, of course, the loss of loved ones will continue to impact us all for some time, but more so the young whose normal course of development has been disrupted. I will continue bringing us back to the long-term effects of the pandemic throughout the book as it is relevant in every chapter.

We have explored some examples of blended states. Even the most calm, grounded person does not live their life solely in their ventral vagal state. We all experience blended states, including the children or young people you work with. Consider now how your week has been so far and see if you can identify some experiences of blended states. We will be exploring reflections on your own autonomic states and identifying the autonomic states of your pupils in later chapters.

Signs of Threat and Signs of Safety

Some signs of threat are obvious and are perceived on a conscious level, such as hearing that sudden loud bang mentioned earlier or feeling a sharp pain in your side. Polyvagal Theory is concerned with the activity of the ANS and our responses to the cues of threat and cues of safety detected by the ANS, so we are going to be focusing on these *unconscious* signs of threat and safety. These signs are below your level of consciousness; in other words, you are *not aware* of them. Your only experience of these signs might be in a sense that something isn't right, a 'sixth sense' or a 'gut feeling'. Have you ever had that feeling that you're being watched when there's no actual evidence that you are? Have you ever had a bad feeling about something, but you can't pinpoint why you have that feeling? These are examples of being tuned in to your ANS.

We can classify cues of threat and safety into three categories:

- internal
- external
- relational

Internal cues of threat or safety come from within the body and external cues from the environment. Relational cues of threat or safety come from interactions and relationships with other people. You may have had the experience of someone making you feel uneasy for no obvious reason, or someone making you feel relaxed and safe, again for no obvious reason. These are from unconscious *relational* signs detected by your ANS. When someone smiles at you, you may be filled with warm feelings, or you may feel uneasy and wary. Your ANS determines how that smile feels to you. Your ANS is an expert at picking up on authenticity and will tell you whether someone's smile is genuine or fake. The unconscious signs your ANS is detecting are coming from the other person's ANS, so neither of you have a conscious awareness of them. As professionals who work with people all day long, we are continuously impacting on other people's autonomic nervous systems, most notably the children and young people in our care. We are radiating *unconscious* signs that tell others about our own state. This is one of the most important concepts I hope to convey in this book:

Your ANS is talking to the ANS of every child or every person you encounter.

Obviously, you want your ANS to be sending cues of safety to the children, but here's the crux: *Incongruence* is read as a sign of threat, which means you cannot fool the child's ANS – you cannot 'fake it'! Giving a fake smile when really you are feeling stressed, will not fool the child into thinking you are happy and relaxed. The child's ANS will know you are stressed, and smiling is incongruent with stress. The incongruence is a sign of threat, so the child's ANS tells the child things aren't OK; something is wrong. Then their sympathetic nervous system is likely to be activated as they ready themselves for the potential threat.

I'm not suggesting you don't smile at your pupils when you are feeling stressed. Instead, I am recommending that by applying your understanding of Polyvagal Theory, you *address your own autonomic state*. Your stress response will then be reduced as you strengthen your ventral vagal state, and reduce any sympathetic mobilisation or dorsal shutdown, and you will be smiling from your ventral vagal state, so it really is an authentic smile. Your ANS is then sending cues of safety to the child's ANS. Later in this book, we will be exploring how you can tune in to your own ANS and manage your autonomic responses to challenging emotions such as stress.

Emotional Regulation

I will be referring in later chapters to children and young people in a state of **dysregulation**, showing how we can help the development of their **self-regulation** and how the communication from your ANS to the child's ANS can result in **co-regulation**, so I feel it would be worth clarifying now what these terms mean.

The regulation of our emotional state can be thought of as experiencing the feeling without becoming overwhelmed by it. When you self-regulate, you manage the feeling, so it does not hijack you, in other words, you stay in control. You are able to step out of the feeling so you can observe it, identify it and then use strategies to keep it at a manageable level.

I was about to give an hour-long presentation on Polyvagal Theory at a conference of nearly a hundred education professionals, and to say I was anxious is an understatement! Sure, I'd held assemblies for three hundred Year 9 pupils before, delivered training in schools and taught some extremely challenging classes, but this was a new experience. I knew if my anxiety overwhelmed me, I wouldn't be able to explain the concepts clearly at all. As I sat watching the speaker before me, I became quite preoccupied with the clock on the wall! As my time to speak got closer, I could feel my breathing become shallow and my heart racing. I sat up straight and tall in my chair and consciously dropped my shoulders, as I took a deep long breath. I clenched and released my hands a few times, wiggled my toes and drank some cold water. I checked through my notes and made sure I had my first few lines clear in my mind to get my started. Then it was time.

> **Through the Polyvagal Lens ...**
>
> *I knew I would be anxious and recognised my anxiety by my body reactions. I could feel the sympathetic mobilisation in my fast shallow breathing and fast heartrate. I also felt tension in my shoulders, hands and feet. These are all 'fight, flight or freeze' responses. But my ventral vagal state was very much online, so I was able to observe the feeling and the body responses and plan a course of action. I stepped back from the anxiety, saw it for what it was, and then used strategies to manage it. I self-regulated my anxiety. The deep breathing, connecting with my body (wiggling my toes and drinking cold water) and relaxing my body were all actions that strengthened my ventral vagal state, effectively sending signals to my sympathetic nervous system to stand down. I was still a little anxious during my presentation, but I could think clearly, communicate effectively and answer questions.*

Self-regulation is sometimes misunderstood as meaning being grounded and relaxed. As Lisa Dion (2018, p. 59) explains: 'Regulation occurs in a moment of mindful awareness. It does not necessarily mean being calm.'

In terms of Polyvagal Theory, self-regulation means keeping your ventral vagal state online *while* the strong feeling might be activating sympathetic mobilisation or dorsal shutdown, as described in the example above. It could also mean bringing yourself back to your ventral vagal state if you have become overwhelmed by an emotion.

> *Beth had had a particularly difficult day at work. She had lost her lunchtime to dealing with a fight in the corridor and ended her day with a challenging phone call from an irate parent. She had just got home from work to find her Amazon parcel sitting in a puddle outside her front door. She huffed as she picked it up and headed inside. There she discovered the 'present' left by her dog on her beloved vintage rug. That was the last straw. Beth threw the wet Amazon parcel on the floor and started shouting and swearing at her startled dog. Then Beth saw her dog cowering and stopped herself. She took a deep breath and took a 'step back' from what was happening. She noticed her face feeling hot and her hands shaking. She recognised her anger, and then felt empathy for her frightened dog. She realised the 'accident' on the rug was most likely due to her being home late. Beth stroked her dog and spoke kindly to her. Beth knew that they would both feel better if they went out for a walk. Breathing the fresh air, connecting positively with her dog and the physical activity all helped reduce her anger, and put everything back in perspective. Once home again, she was able to clean up the rug, email Amazon about the damaged parcel, phone a friend to talk through the challenges at work and then settle down for the evening.*
>
> **Through the Polyvagal Lens ...**
>
> *Beth had experienced other people's anger during her day which would have taken its toll on her ANS. She likely experienced some sympathetic mobilisation when*

> dealing with the fight and the angry parent, leaving her with a weakened ventral vagal state. The unfortunate incidents once home then caused anger to overwhelm her. Sympathetic mobilisation had started to take over. However, she hadn't completely lost control. The recognition of another's feelings and sense of empathy happens in the neocortex, which is only active with ventral vagal activation, so her ventral vagal state was still online, even if only a little. Her ventral vagal state strengthened when she empathised with her dog as her social engagement system activated. She was then able to step back, recognise and identify her anger, and use strategies to manage it. Her sympathetic mobilisation reduced. Beth had every right to feel angry after the day she'd had, but her dog didn't deserve her wrath. Beth self-regulated to bring her anger under control, then used the energy of the anger to take a calm course of action once she was home from their walk.

If your ventral vagal state has been deactivated and sympathetic mobilisation or dorsal shutdown have taken over, then you are dysregulated, meaning you have been overwhelmed by the emotion. Everyone experiences dysregulation from time to time, and as humans we have a go-to strategy to help bring us back: social engagement. By connecting with another person, we seek out their support to co-regulate us. They effectively lend us their ventral vagal state to help us bring our emotional state back under control.

Another scenario helps us see this in action:

> It was Year 10 mock exam week, and maths teacher, Steve, was dreading his last lesson of the day – 10X5. Bottom set, various behavioural problems, and several special education needs. It was always a tough lesson, but today he would be trying to enforce exam conditions. He just wanted the day to be over. It was lunchtime and Steve was struggling to relax in the staffroom. He found himself pacing, wringing his hands, and wishing he hadn't quit smoking. He started shaking his head and muttering, 'I can't do it, I just can't do it.' He knew there was one person who might help him calm down and headed for her office. Jan was on the phone, so Steve paced up and down the corridor, peering through her door window as he passed it, then burst in as soon as he spotted her putting the phone down.
>
> 'Jan, I can't teach 10X5 today! How can I get them to be quiet for a whole hour for their mock? They've never managed more than five minutes! I can't do it! I just want to go home,' he blurted.
>
> Jan immediately picked up on his panic and urged him to sit down as she made him a hot drink. She encouraged him to talk through his anxieties and fears, as she listened attentively. Her face conveyed empathy, as she nodded and held eye-contact with him. They explored worse case scenarios, and Steve felt his panic subside as he put a new perspective on the situation. As the bell rang, marking the end of lunch, Steve stood up making himself tall, took a deep breath, smiled at Jan and said,
>
> 'Thanks Jan. Wish me luck!'

Through the Polyvagal Lens ...

Steve was clearly in sympathetic mobilisation, with his feelings of dread, fear and panic causing physiological changes in his body, ready for 'fight, flight or freeze'. He still had some ventral vagal activation, as he was still able to think, but unfortunately his thought processes were not helpful, as he was telling himself that he wouldn't be able to manage. One thought, however, did help – seeking social engagement to co-regulate his overwhelming feelings. Jan offered physical suggestions to calm his body (sitting down and the hot drink), and unconscious cues of safety in her facial expressions, eye-contact and calm demeanour. By the end of their conversation, the situation facing Steve had not changed at all, but his response to it had. His sympathetic mobilisation had reduced significantly, and he was firmly in his ventral vagal state, thanks to the impact of Jan's ANS radiating cues of safety.

What Steve may not have realised was that his stronger ventral vagal state would have caused his ANS to send cues of safety to the pupils of 10X5. The lesson would have been somewhat easier as a result. If he had taken the lesson while in sympathetic mobilisation, his ANS would have been sending cues of threat to his pupils' ANS, sending them into sympathetic mobilisation – a recipe for disaster.

As infants, we begin our journey to developing self-regulation through co-regulation from our parents. Repeated experiences of our emotional state being co-regulated teach us that our feelings are manageable and don't have to overwhelm us. We continue learning to self-regulate throughout childhood and into adulthood, and even as adults we still occasionally need co-regulation.

Children learn self-regulation through co-regulation from all the adults in their lives, but especially from the adults they see frequently, such as teaching staff.

Four-year-old Sanjay was playing outside at school. He was engrossed in rolling his favourite toy car along the ground, making his best vroom-vroom noises, when seemingly out of nowhere, Callum snatched the car, shouting, 'Mine!'

Sanjay jumped up and tried grabbing the car back, growling angrily, 'It's not your turn!'

Callum gave Sanjay a push and ran off with the car.

Sanjay burst into tears and ran over to Mrs Lipman. Unable to express himself clearly with words, he simply pointed in the direction of Callum and whimpered 'My car ...'. Mrs Lipman lowered herself to Sanjay's height, took his hand and comforted him with reassuring words, then walked him over to Callum to resolve the conflict. Sanjay stopped crying. He watched Mrs Lipman intently as she spoke to the boys and listened carefully to what she was saying. She validated their feelings, then talked about sharing and taking turns, and made it clear that it was not OK to push or hurt other children. Callum said sorry, and with support, the boys came to an agreement about taking turns playing with the car.

Through the Polyvagal Lens ...

Sanjay was in his ventral vagal state while playing, but quickly became overwhelmed by his feelings during the altercation. He was angry and upset at the car being snatched away from him and frightened by the physical attack. Sympathetic mobilisation was activated. Initially he experienced a blend of ventral vagal with sympathetic mobilisation as he was able to express in words his feelings of injustice to Callum. However, sympathetic mobilisation took over when Callum pushed him, leading to a 'flight' response. He ran away to safety, i.e., Mrs Lipman. At only 4 years old, Sanjay had not yet developed the skills to self-regulate in such a challenging situation and needed co-regulation from a trusted adult. Mrs Lipman used her secure ventral vagal state to provide Sanjay with conscious and unconscious cues of safety, which brought Sanjay back to his ventral vagal state. She used reassuring words, body language, tone of voice and facial expressions. It's worth noting what was happening for Callum in this incident. He was likely to have been in sympathetic mobilisation as he was verbally and physically aggressive towards Sanjay. In mediating the conflict with a clear calm approach, Mrs Lipman co-regulated both children.

Summary

Learning Points

- Polyvagal Theory explains how we respond to experiences in terms of the activity of the autonomic nervous system (ANS).
- The ANS detects unconscious cues of safety and cues of threat, which then determine the autonomic state.
- There are three autonomic states: ventral vagal, sympathetic mobilisation and dorsal shutdown.
- Ventral vagal is the state of calm and safety, associated with social engagement.
- Sympathetic mobilisation is the first line of defence against potential threat, and is associated with the 'fight, flight or freeze' response.
- Dorsal shutdown is the second line of defence when sympathetic mobilisation is ineffective in finding safety, and results in collapse, psychological disconnection, and physiological shutdown.
- Much of the time, we experience blended states and are therefore able to reflect on our own ANS activity and develop the self-awareness to strengthen our ventral vagal state.
- Throughout childhood, we develop the capacity for emotional self-regulation through effective co-regulation from care-givers, including teaching staff.
- We become dysregulated when we are overwhelmed by our emotional state, and then need self-regulation or co-regulation to bring us back to a regulated emotional state.

- The ANS of one person communicates on an unconscious level with the ANS of another person, thereby influencing their autonomic state, which can result in co-regulation or dysregulation.

Practical Exercise

Notice right now what is happening in your body in terms of your *heartrate, breathing, body sensations* and *body tension*. Are you able to *think clearly* at the moment? What *emotions* are you feeling right now? Try this a few times today to identify which autonomic state you are in. You might find yourself in a blended state. Note down what you notice as the *signs* of the autonomic state you are in.

2 Polyvagal Theory and Child Development

This chapter applies **Polyvagal Theory** to some child development theories, which you may well have heard of or studied. We will be discussing the theories of Piaget, Erikson, Vygotsky, and Bowlby, and also briefly considering the contributions to our understanding of child development from Klein and Winnicott. **Attachment Theory** will be explored in some detail as it is so pertinent to the work of school staff in supporting the emotional wellbeing of pupils.

By considering theories of child development alongside Polyvagal Theory, we can explore how the **autonomic nervous system** (ANS) is shaped by the child's early experiences. We will look at the child development theories most relevant to education: Jean Piaget's Theory of Cognitive Development, Lev Vygotsky's Sociocultural Theory, Erik Erikson's Theory of Psychosocial Development and John Bowlby's Attachment Theory. Such well-established theories, seen through the lens of Polyvagal Theory, can provide us with a clearer picture of how the child grows and develops.

Piaget: Cognitive Development Theory

The Swiss psychologist, Jean Piaget, developed the **Cognitive Development Theory** to explain how children learn. His theory states that the child's brain develops in four stages (Piaget and Inhelder, 1969):

1. *The Sensorimotor Stage* - birth to 2 years: the infant constructs an understanding of the world through sensory experiences (for instance, what they hear, see, smell, taste, and touch) and physical actions (such as moving their arms and legs, gripping things with their hands, making sounds, facial expressions, etc.).
2. *The Preoperational Stage* - 2-7 years: the child starts to represent the world symbolically through words and images (using language and drawing pictures, etc.).
3. *The Concrete Operational Stage* - 7-11 years: the child develops the ability to reason logically (meaning they can master maths and science concepts more easily).
4. *The Formal Operational Stage* - 11 years to adulthood: the adolescent develops the ability to use abstract ideas and more complex thought processes (such as hypothesising, reflecting, and considering future possibilities).

DOI: 10.4324/9781003396574-4

The study of stages 2-4 is useful when considering the approach to teaching skills and under-standing for both primary and secondary-aged children, as these stages relate to the child's acquisition of language, use of symbolic thinking, and development of logic and abstract thinking. Each stage depends on the progress made in the stage before, so disruptions early in the child's cognitive development have an impact on later learning. Sue Gascoyne, in her book, *Messy Play in the Early Years*, explores in detail the importance of sensory play, with reference to Piagetian development. As she explains, 'In the Pre, Concrete and Formal Operations stages too, encounters with messy resources give children sensations like cold, slimy and soft, underpinning language and supporting the development of children's thinking ...' (Gascoyne, 2019, p. 21).

When thinking about Polyvagal Theory, we are most interested in the first stage. Piaget's Sensorimotor Stage explains how an infant first starts understanding the world through sen-sory experience and physical actions, in other words, through the central nervous system.

Six-month-old Rosie is sitting in her highchair with food on a plastic plate in front of her. She reaches for something green that she hasn't seen before, closes her fingers around it and instinctively puts it in her mouth. She feels that this new thing is cool and wet. She enjoys the sensations in her mouth and the new taste. She reaches for another piece. Rosie then notices her mother sit down next to her and looks towards her. Rosie's mother smiles and says, 'So you like cucumber, then?' Rosie smiles back at her mum and holds out her hand with fingers covered in half-eaten cucumber. She makes a bab-bling sound that her mother knows to be a happy sound.

Through the Polyvagal Lens ...

Rosie's central nervous system is developing rapidly at this age. She is compelled to seek new sensory experiences to learn about the world around her. She has already learned a connection between the physical actions of reaching for some-thing, gripping it, and bringing it to her mouth, and the sensory input of touch and taste inside her mouth. She uses this connection frequently, so her mother is con-stantly checking that Rosie isn't putting anything unsuitable in her mouth. Rosie has also developed a strong connection with her mother, where they exchange smiles and take turns 'talking' to each other. We can tell that Rosie and her mother are both in their ventral vagal states, as they are communicating effectively with facial expressions, with body language, and verbally. In other words, their social engagement systems are active.

A child who has not progressed sufficiently through the first stage may seek sensory experi-ences, such as making mess, to address this gap in their development. If and when this need is met, they should then progress more smoothly through the next stages. Thinking about the chil-dren and young people you work with, are there any who seem to want to make mess whenever there is an opportunity, such as with paints or water? These children may not have completely moved through their first Piagetian stage and may need to revisit the sensorimotor experience. Are there structured opportunities for mess-making that you can plan for these children?

Erikson: Psychosocial Development Theory

Erik Erikson gave another theory on stages of development, but unlike Piaget, who focused on *cognitive* development, Erikson's theory concentrates more on *social* factors. Erikson's **Psychosocial Development Theory** has eight stages which take us from birth, through the development in childhood and adolescence, then into stages of adulthood (Erikson and Erikson, 1997). As we are only considering child development here, I will only be referring to the first five stages (Figure 2.1).

Erikson's theory of psychosocial development emphasizes the importance of an infant's early experience of *trust* in the parent, leading to a sense of autonomy as the child grows. This trust is established through the parent tuning in (or 'attuning') to the infant's emotional state and soothing them when distressed, in other words, providing the infant with repeated experiences of returning to their ventral vagal state. According to Erikson, if the child has missed out on the experience of building trust, they will likely move down the path of *mistrust* leading to *shame, guilt, inferiority,* and *identity confusion*. Unless, of course, adults in the child's life invest time in nurturing the child's sense of *trust*, transferring them back onto the path of *autonomy, initiative, industry,* and *identity*.

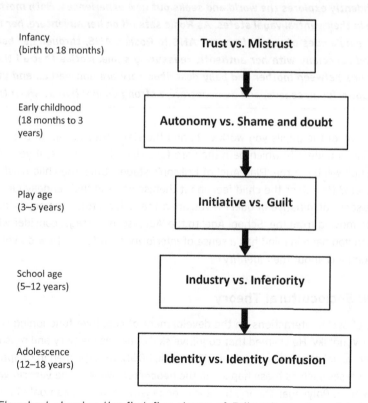

Figure 2.1 Flowchart showing the first five stages of Erikson's psychosocial development theory

A few months on, and little Rosie has mastered crawling. Her mother has taken her to a local playgroup. Rosie is sitting on her mother's lap looking around, when she spots something big and colourful across the room. Rosie wriggles and squirms in her mother's arms and makes a small whining noise. Her mother gently places her on the floor. Rosie crawls across the room at quite a pace, towards the new exciting colourful thing. She stops briefly and turns to look at her mum, who smiles encouragingly. Rosie resumes her quest and makes her way to the little inflated paddling pool full of brightly coloured balls.

Through the Polyvagal Lens ...

Rosie is exploring the world further now as she is mobile, and able to move towards things that interest her, however, she cannot yet express herself with words. Rosie's mother is attuned to Rosie's feelings and needs. She understands Rosie's communication that she wants to be on the floor, and after a quick assessment of any possible risks, she lifts her down. Watching Rosie crawl towards the ball-pit, her mother realises that this will be an exciting new experience for Rosie and responds with reassurance when Rosie seems a little unsure. Rosie trusts her mother to understand her and meet her needs. She is moving into Erikson's second stage of autonomy as she confidently explores the world and seeks out new experiences. Both mother and baby are in their ventral vagal states. As Rosie sets off on her adventure, her mother provides ample cues of safety from her ANS to Rosie's ANS, through her body language and especially with her authentic reassuring smile. Notice that all the communications between mother and baby described here are non-verbal, and yet they provide powerful messages, and demonstrate a strong connection between the two.

Consider one of the pupils you work with, and the stage they are at on the flowchart in Figure 2.1. Can you identify which path they are following? For instance, if you are a Year 1 LSA, your pupil will be in the 'Play Age' of Erikson's stages. Does the child *trust* the adults caring for them? How does the child feel about themselves and their endeavours? Does the child have a sense of *initiative* or *guilt*? If you are a Year 7 form tutor, the pupils in your tutor group will be moving from the 'School Age' to the 'Adolescence' stage, consider whether the young person you have in mind has a sense of *inferiority* or *industry*. How do you think this young person feels about their *identity*?

Vygotsky: Sociocultural Theory

The impact of social interactions on the development of cognitive functioning was put forward by Lev Vygotsky. He claimed that cognitive skills, such as memory and reasoning originate through social relations and culture (Santrock, 2001). As explained in Chapter 1, higher thinking processes such as these happen in the **neocortex**, while in the **ventral vagal state**. As we know from Polyvagal Theory, the social engagement system can only function when the neocortex is functioning well, in other words, when in the ventral vagal state.

For the developing child, this means that positive social interactions are critical for the healthy development of their neocortex and strengthening of their ventral vagal state. In infancy, these interactions come primarily through parents and close family members. At school, the focus of social interactions is through relationships with peers and staff. Vygotsky's theory supports the use of group work in the classroom, as it suggests that positive interactions between pupils helps the development of their cognitive processes and therefore the learning of new skills.

Jack is in his Year 8 English lesson and the class have been instructed to work in small groups, identifying metaphors in a piece of text. Jack shuffles his chair towards his group - Gemma, Priya, and Lucas. They acknowledge each other with brief eye-contact and subtle facial expressions. Jack is a little wary of Lucas, who always seems to be in trouble for not getting on with his work. He glances at the sketches Lucas seems to be absorbed in. Priya starts reading aloud the first paragraph of the text, then says 'Metaphors?' looking in Jack's direction. Jack responds with what he thinks might be a good contribution. Gemma declares 'I'll write down our ideas' and starts noting down what Jack has said. He smiles and adds a little more to his idea. Priya looks at Lucas and asks what he thinks. Lucas looks up from his doodling and mutters 'I don't know.' Jack proposes that Lucas reads the second paragraph of the text, which he reluctantly agrees to. Once finished, Lucas nervously suggests a metaphor from the text he's just read. Gemma smiles, says, 'Good one, Lucas' and jots down his idea. Lucas looks down and continues his doodling, with a bashful smile.

Through the Polyvagal Lens ...

It would seem that the girls were in their ventral vagal states, as they confidently took the initiative in the group task. Jack's ANS was picking up some potential cues of threat from Lucas' ANS, causing him to feel wary, but his ventral vagal state was strong as he was able to think clearly and communicate well during the task. Jack was in a blended state, but predominantly ventral vagal. This was not the case for Lucas, who may have been feeling threatened by the difficulty of the task and/or the risk of humiliation in front of his peers. His ANS was detecting cues of threat from the situation, which caused a degree of dorsal shutdown as he tried to avoid the task and gave a minimal response when asked to contribute. Jack's ANS sent Lucas' ANS cues of safety when he suggested Lucas read the paragraph, as this was a less-threatening activity than identifying metaphors. Jack had activated Lucas' social engagement system, thereby strengthening Lucas' ventral vagal state. Lucas then had the confidence to take the risk of suggesting a metaphor. The positive feedback from Gemma then further strengthened both Jack and Lucas' ventral vagal states. These young people, through working as a group, exchanged cues of safety between their autonomic nervous systems and so strengthened each other's ventral vagal states, which resulted in a more productive learning experience for all of them.

Thinking about your pupils, can you identify any who appear to struggle with social interactions and also seem to be underachieving? Consider how regular carefully planned group activities might help these children, in light of Vygotsky's theory. Of course, the outcome of the group work described above would not have been as positive if all the young people in the group had been in the state Lucas had started in. There needed to be stronger cues of safety within the group than cues of threat, in order for the shift to stronger ventral vagal states. Consider the group dynamics of the individual groups your pupils work in. Are there any groups where very little learning happens, and there is a sense of counterproductive social interactions? Consider how planning who works with who could provide stronger cues of safety within the group.

Bowlby: Attachment Theory

John Bowlby's **Attachment Theory** is one that many education professionals are familiar with. We will be looking in more detail at this theory, as it so relevant in the work we do as educators in supporting the emotional wellbeing of our pupils.

Bowlby proposed the idea that a baby builds a strong attachment to the person who is meeting their survival needs, such as food, warmth, and protection. He referred to this relationship, usually with the infant's mother, as the **secure base** (Bowlby, 1969). For a secure attachment, the mother also provides *containment* for the child's overwhelming feelings, by responding with empathy, understanding and sensitivity. As the child becomes mobile, they start to explore the world, in the comforting knowledge that they can return to their secure base. This gives the child a sense of safety and confidence when exploring and trying new things. Once the child is old enough to start school, the school itself can become the child's secure base, where their physical and emotional needs are met with empathy and understanding.

In terms of Polyvagal Theory, this secure base relationship with their mother provides the infant's ANS with frequent cues of safety whenever they feel overwhelmed by their feelings or body sensations (such as hunger, cold or tiredness). Sensations such as these are threats to the baby's survival as they cannot feed themselves or warm themselves up; they are utterly dependent on their parents to keep them alive. Therefore, many body sensations and feelings are read by the baby's ANS as cues of threat to their survival, and the **sympathetic mobilisation** system is quickly activated. The baby's body tenses up, their arms and legs flail and they make as much noise as possible to attract the attention of their attachment figure. This is the only survival strategy the baby has. A sensitive well-attuned mother, in providing the secure base, repeatedly responds empathically to the baby's cries, and soothes the baby with holding, feeding, a calming voice, smiles, etc. The baby's ANS is flooded with cues of safety, and they are brought back to their ventral vagal state. Quite an emotional rollercoaster for the baby, but with a parent who is attuned to the baby's needs, the soothing is effective, and with time, the infant starts to learn that their feelings do not have to overwhelm them. Through this co-regulation from the parent, the child starts to develop their ability to self-regulate. It is worth noting here that the baby does not need a perfect parent, in order for them to experience a secure base, the baby needs a parent who is attuned enough, sensitive enough, empathic enough and provides enough of these repeated experiences of co-regulation.

The infant learns **attachment behaviours** depending on the quality of the attachment to their mother. Attachment behaviours serve the purpose of seeking proximity and contact with the attachment figure. In her book, *Attachment in the Classroom*, which I highly recommend, Heather Geddes explains the implications for the quality of the attachment, 'as an organiser of behaviour towards others in ways that persist into adult life, affecting later relationships and choices' (Geddes, 2006, p. 40).

An attachment which is not secure, giving the infant an experience of uncontained emotions, and/or physical needs being unmet, causes the child to learn extreme attachment behaviours which they later bring to school. We will look at these behaviours in more detail as we explore the three different *insecure* attachment patterns.

There are four attachment styles in total described by Bowlby, which are determined by the child's earliest experiences with their caregiver:

- Secure Attachment
- Insecure Attachment: Ambivalent
- Insecure Attachment: Avoidant
- Insecure Attachment: Disorganised

These attachment styles will be explained here as four distinct forms, however, it should be noted that human behaviour can never be classified in such simple terms. Children usually have more than one attachment figure, and may experience different attachment styles with each parent, therefore their attachment style is not so clear-cut. There may also be changes in the primary attachment figure themselves with life events, such as a bereavement, or changes in family circumstances, causing the child to have a different primary carer, such as parents separating. The attachment styles are experienced on a continuum, with severe cases and moderate cases of each style, and there can also be some overlap. We will be exploring extreme examples here to emphasise the differences between the attachment styles.

Secure Attachment

The secure attachment is provided by the attachment figure who is attuned to the child's needs and responds with empathy, sensitivity and understanding. The securely attached child has a good enough experience of a secure base for them to feel safe as they go out into the world. They trust that the adult caring for them will meet their needs and keep them physically and emotionally safe, even when that adult is a new teacher whom they've only just met. This child knows their ventral vagal state well, and has learnt effective ways to return to it, whenever they experience cues of threat.

The attachment behaviours of the securely attached mobile infant, such as a toddler, include the following:

- Crying when their mother is absent, but easily being soothed by another known adult or when reunited with their mother
- Moving towards their mother and seeking physical contact when feeling uncertain about a new situation

- Making eye-contact with their mother for reassurance when trying something new
- Moving towards their mother to communicate needs, such as hunger, thirst, or pain

In school, the securely attached child or teenager may show behaviours such as:

- Following school routines and rules
- Seeking out adult support when feeling emotionally or physically unsafe
- Taking measured risks, such as performing in a school play
- Working independently when required to
- Working in groups with some degree of self-confidence
- Forming and maintaining healthy friendships

Little Rosie is now 18 months old. She is walking, starting to talk, and exploring the world around her. Rosie's mother needs to go to work but is not able to leave Rosie with her usual child-minder, so arranges for her friend, Tina, to look after Rosie. Tina is an adult Rosie knows quite well but she has never been left alone with her before. Rosie's mother spends a few minutes settling Rosie on the floor at Tina's house, with some toys from home, then says goodbye to Rosie and leaves. Rosie watches her mum leave and starts whimpering, looking towards the closed door. She gets up and heads towards the door, her arm outreached, saying, 'Mum-mum ... mum.' Tina kneels next to Rosie, gently takes her hand, and says in a soft but animated voice, 'Rosie, I have something exciting to show you – would you like to see my goldfish?' Rosie stops and looks at Tina's kind smiling face. She points at the door and says, 'Mum-mum' to Tina. Tina comforts Rosie, with eye-contact and a soothing voice 'Mummy will be back soon, Rosie.' She picks Rosie up and says, 'Let's go see those fish.' Rosie tries out the new word 'ish'. 'That's right, fish!' encourages Tina, as she carries her to the fish tank. They entertain themselves watching the fish, and the rest of Rosie's time with Tina goes smoothly. When Rosie's mother returns, Rosie runs towards her and into her arms, then in her gabbled speech, she tells her about the fish and the other exciting things that have happened at Tina's house.

Let's fast forward. Rosie is now 11 years old and about to start her first day in secondary school. Over breakfast, she tells her mum that she feels nervous and excited. She talks about worrying that she might get lost, then reassures herself with the plan that she will stick with her friend, Chloe. Rosie's mother smiles as she listens to Rosie declaring problems then solving them herself! When she drops Rosie off outside the school, she smiles again as she watches Rosie take a deep breath before opening the car door. 'You'll be fine, sweetie', she says reassuringly. Rosie heads into the school, pausing briefly to look back at her mum, who smiles in that comforting way that Rosie knows so well. In the tutor room, Mrs Thompson, whom the children met in the Year 6 transition week back in the summer term, greets the class with a warm smile and starts taking the register. Rosie sits herself next to Chloe, then smiles at Mrs Thompson, as she says 'Here, Miss', when her name is called.

> ## Through the Polyvagal Lens ...
>
> *We know Rosie quite well now, and we can see how her secure attachment to her mother helped her manage their separation on both occasions. Rosie was able to transfer her secure base experience to Tina and later to Mrs Thompson. Rosie's mother provided her with containment for her feelings when she was an infant, so Rosie learnt that her feelings were manageable. This gave Rosie a strong ventral vagal state. Rosie was easily co-regulated by Tina, as the secure attachment to her mother had provided Rosie with a strong ventral vagal state. Through repeated experiences of co-regulation, Rosie developed the capacity for self-regulation. When talking through her worries about starting a new school, Rosie was able to identify her feelings and self-regulate her feeling of anxiety. Rosie's worry about getting lost did not weaken her ventral vagal state, as she was able to use the higher thought process of problem solving (in her neocortex) to come up with a plan. Rosie intuitively knew that taking a deep breath would help calm her nerves before she opened the car door, as she had a strong connection with her own body and knew what it needed. Once in the tutor room, we can see that Rosie's social engagement system was active as she sought out her friend to sit with and interacted confidently with her teacher. Rosie showed a solid connection to others and to herself. The secure attachment with her mother enabled Rosie to develop the capacity to self-regulate, to maintain her ventral vagal state and to approach new experiences with confidence, self-assurance and trust in the adults caring for her.*

If you consider the pupils you work with, you may be able to identify those who have a more secure attachment by thinking about the attachment behaviours described above but remember that attachment styles are on a continuum. At the other end of the spectrum are the insecure attachments, of which there are three types: *ambivalent*, *avoidant*, and *disorganised*.

Ambivalent Attachment

The insecure **ambivalent attachment** style involves the experience of an unreliable attachment figure, who lacks sensitivity for their baby's needs. The mother seeks closeness to the infant to meet *their own* needs rather than the needs of the child. The mother does not attune to the needs of the infant, and therefore is unreliable in meeting their needs. The child seeks proximity and contact, as they need it for survival, but they find no security or emotional containment from their attachment figure. This type of response from the mother is sometimes referred to as *intrusive* or *enmeshed*.

In Polyvagal Theory terms, when the infant is distressed, their ANS continues to feel cues of threat, and they stay in sympathetic mobilisation, even with contact from their mother. The mother's ANS is not providing cues of safety for the infant. This child learns that feelings *are* overwhelming. They don't experience enough co-regulation and therefore develop limited capacity for self-regulation. This child learns to be anxious and later brings that anxiety with them to school. They haven't had a secure base from which to explore the world with confidence and safety. This child does not trust that a secure base, such as their class teacher, will be able to help them regulate their overwhelming emotions.

An infant with an ambivalent attachment style might do the following:

- Be distressed when their mother is absent, but not reassured or comforted by her return
- Be clingy with their mother
- Cry and whine more than other infants of the same age

At school, this child might show the following attachment behaviours:

- Show signs of extreme separation anxiety and generally high levels of anxiety
- Attempts to control others, including teaching staff
- Care-seeking behaviours in lessons
- A sense of helplessness and dependence on the teacher
- Aggression directed towards the teacher when frustrated
- Somatised (physically experienced) responses to anxiety, e.g., stomach aches, headaches
- Limited tolerance of the anxiety related to transitions, such as moving from primary to secondary school
- Poor response to boundaries and rules
- Poor attendance

Maya is 3 months old. She is being held in her mother's arms on the sofa at home. Maya has just been fed after waking from a sleep. She is wide awake and alert. There is a colourful playmat on the floor nearby that Maya is looking at. She reaches out with her arms, her hands open. Her mother finds a firmer grip and tries to bounce her on her knee, saying 'There, there.' Maya then struggles in her mother's arms, moving her arms and legs. Her mother holds her tighter. Maya arches her back and pushes against her mother with her legs. Her mother holds her close to her body, then gets up and walks about rocking Maya in her arms. Maya starts to cry and continues arching her back. Her mother sits down with her again and offers her more milk. Maya turns her head away, crying. After a while, Maya's mother tries putting Maya on the playmat, but by this time, Maya is screaming. Maya continues crying as her mother sits over her looking into her face, trying to distract her with the dangling toys over the playmat. Eventually Maya stops crying and reaches towards the toys. A few minutes later, her mother picks her up again and carries her around the house, rocking her.

Seven years later and Maya is walking to school with her mum. At the school gate, Maya's mum hugs her tightly and tells her it won't be long until she can come home and not to worry. Maya starts whimpering and tells her mum she doesn't want to go to school today. She starts saying she has tummy ache and can't go in. The LSA for Maya's class, Miss Bailey, follows her established routine of meeting Maya at the gate, and taking her hand to walk her to the classroom. Once in the classroom, she distracts Maya with some colouring, so she doesn't notice her mother through the window, still standing at the gate. The lesson starts, and the class teacher, Mr Howe, starts explaining the first numeracy task to the children. Maya walks over to Miss Bailey whilst Mr Howe is talking to the class and says she can't do the numeracy task and her hand hurts.

Mr Howe asks Maya to sit back down in her place. Maya does so reluctantly, then puts her hand up as soon as he starts talking to the class again. 'Yes, Maya', says Mr Howe. 'I can't do it', moans Maya. Mr Howe points out that he hasn't finished explaining the task yet. He doesn't get to finish explaining before Maya has interrupted him three more times, with irrelevant comments or pleas for help.

Through the Polyvagal Lens …

Maya's mother was not attuned to Maya's needs. She did not recognise that Maya was trying to get out of her hold, and that she needed time and space to experiment with her body movements. Although she had a playmat for Maya, she seemed unable or unwilling to let Maya experience it, without her intense involvement. Maya's ANS was detecting cues of threat from her mother in the form of unmet needs and lack of co-regulation. Maya's ANS then moved her into sympathetic mobilisation and her body responded with movements of 'fight' or 'flight'. Maya's early experiences with her mother taught her that feelings are overwhelming. Due to her mother's intense intrusive involvement, Maya never learnt that her own feelings are separate from her mother's feelings, which is an important stage of development for an infant. She learnt to be in a constant state of anxiety. The lack of co-regulation resulted in poor self-regulation for 7-year-old Maya, who could not manage her separation anxiety at the school gate, which was being fed by her mother's overwhelming separation anxiety. In the classroom, Maya experienced further separation anxiety, which drove her attachment behaviour of constantly seeking attention from the adults caring for her.

I think every teacher or professional working with children and young people will have come across 'attention-seeking' behaviours. It's worth remembering where these behaviours have come from and how they are an attempt at regulating overwhelming feelings of anxiety in the young person. We can think of all behaviours as forms of communication of dysregulated emotions or unmet needs. Consider one or two examples of challenging behaviour you have dealt with in the last week or so. What was the behaviour communicating to you? Was it attachment behaviour? Was it an attempt to regulate an overwhelming emotion, in other words, an attempt to return to the ventral vagal state?

Avoidant Attachment

The insecure **avoidant attachment** style is seen when the infant is rejected by their attachment figure. These infants learn that they have to be self-sufficient and independent because the adults won't help them. Of course, a baby *cannot* be independent, and cannot survive on its own, so is compelled to seek closeness to their mother, but at the same time, their experience of that closeness is a painful rejection. In some cases, the mother becomes angry at her child for needing her attention. So, the infant is caught in an 'approach-avoidance' conflict which gets worse with every experience and is impossible for the infant to resolve. This child both desires and dreads closeness to their mother.

For this infant, the rejection from their mother is read as a threat by their ANS, as they cannot survive without her, therefore, they are moved into their sympathetic mobilisation state. They do not experience cues of safety from their mother's ANS, so they are not brought into their ventral vagal state, in other words, they are not co-regulated. The feeling of life-threatening rejection may become so overwhelming for this child, especially if they are also met with the mother's anger, that they could move into the second line of defence against threat: **dorsal shutdown**. In order to protect themselves from the psychological pain of feeling unwanted and unlovable, the child may cut themselves off from their emotional world. This child may experience a blended state of sympathetic mobilisation and dorsal shutdown, as they may be hypervigilant to the adult's proximity, while also being shut off from their feelings.

The attachment behaviours of an infant with an avoidant attachment style may include the following:

- Little to no signs of distress when separated from their mother and no signs of comfort when she returns
- Not responding when called by their mother
- Expressing feelings of anger and aggression towards toys
- Avoiding looking towards the mother or moving towards her

In school, the child or teenager with an avoidant attachment style may show the following behaviours:

- Not ask for help when they need it, and work very independently
- Have very few or no friends, tending to play alone
- Present as somewhat robotic, showing little emotion in their work or responses, for instance, when reading emotive text in English lessons
- Seem hostile towards others
- Have a sense of unexpressed rage, which may cause other children or young people to keep their distance

Meet 3-week-old Richie. Lying in his cot, Richie is crying. It's some time since he was last fed, and he has just woken up. Richie's mother is in the kitchen, but Richie doesn't know this. He just knows that he has an uncomfortable sensation in his body, so he cries as an instinctive response to this 'bad' feeling. Nobody comes. Richie continues crying for some time, then slowly stops and lies in his cot, quite still, staring ahead. A little while later, his mother comes in, picks him up and feeds him in silence. Richie looks towards his mother, searching for her eyes, but her attention is on her mobile phone screen, and she doesn't look at him.

Richie, now 4 years old, is about to start school. His mother walks with him to the Reception classroom, where they are greeted by Mrs Walsh. Neither Richie nor his mother make eye-contact with Mrs Walsh as she says hello. Richie reaches out and touches his mother's leg. She steps away, turns and leaves. He wanders into the room, without a second glance in his mother's direction, and starts playing with some small toy cars, seemingly oblivious to the presence of the other children already playing with the cars. Mrs Walsh, having failed to connect with Richie when he arrived, calls his name. No response. She walks over to him and sits alongside him as he plays. She says his name again, but still no response. He violently crashes the cars into each other then gets up and wanders to another area of the room. Mrs Walsh decides to give him some space but keeps a close eye on him. Later she notices Richie hurt his foot when climbing outside in the play area. He stumbles to a hiding place behind a hedge. Concerned for his wellbeing, Mrs Walsh seeks him out. She calls his name and says that she's worried that he's hurt himself, as she walks slowly behind the hedge. As soon as Richie sees Mrs Walsh, he starts throwing stones at her and shouts 'Go away!'

Through the Polyvagal Lens ...

Richie's mother did not attune to his needs and seemed to be unwilling or unable to even try. Richie woke up with a sensation that sent him into sympathetic mobilisation as his ANS read the feeling as a cue of threat. With no-one meeting his needs, or co-regulating him to bring him back to his ventral vagal state, his ANS took him down to the next line of defence – dorsal shutdown. His mother might have been under the impression that he was fine when he stopped crying, but it is not normal for a hungry baby to lie still and quiet. His body was starting to shut down. Luckily his mother fed him in time to bring him out of dorsal shutdown and his social engagement system came online as he sought out eye-contact from his mother. With little to no interactions with his mother, Richie's social engagement system was left underdeveloped and his ventral vagal state lacking in stability. Richie learnt from his mother that other people are not sources of safety or security and would not be able to meet his needs or understand his feelings. He had no trust whatsoever in his teacher and relied on himself when hurt. Hiding and throwing stones are both responses of the sympathetic mobilisation state (fight and flight). Richie felt under threat and dysregulated by his feelings, but with an underdeveloped social engagement system, he was not able to seek comfort from another person. As an infant, Richie learnt who he is and what the world is like from his mother. She taught him that nobody cares about him, nobody likes him, and nobody wants him.

This form of attachment can easily be confused with autism, as there is a strong tendency for the young person to avoid social interactions, including eye-contact, and a sense that they are struggling to understand their emotional state. Due to the overlap in signs of attachment disorder and signs of autism, the strategies used by teaching staff to help an autistic child would also benefit a child with this form of insecure attachment, such as predictability in the structure of the day, consistency in the teacher's approach and support in social development and emotional literacy. We will look more closely at autism and other neurodevelopmental conditions though the Polyvagal lens in Chapter 4.

Disorganised Attachment

In the ambivalent and avoidant insecure attachment styles, the attachment behaviours have a level of *organisation* due to the consistent response from the mother – even when that response might be intrusive or rejecting. Insecure **disorganised attachment** style is so called because there is no pattern to the response of the parent, and since the infant has no idea what to expect, they form no pattern to their attachment behaviours. This type of attachment style is sometimes called a *chaotic* insecure attachment. The experience for the infant is of a mother who responds with an unpredictable mix of rejection, anger, physical attack, emotional neglect, and physical neglect. This is the most troublesome child in the school setting because they have no experience of feeling safe and calm. They don't expect the school to keep them physically or emotionally safe and are permanently on high alert for danger. This child is likely to have experienced one or more forms of abuse (emotional abuse, physical abuse, sexual abuse, or neglect). We will explore the impact of abuse in more detail in Chapter 3.

In terms of Polyvagal Theory, this child is likely to have little experience of their ventral vagal state and may be constantly yo-yoing between sympathetic mobilisation and complete dorsal shutdown, or a blended state of the two. They will have experienced very little safety and therefore their ANS will be underdeveloped in its ability to recognise cues of safety. The child's ANS will be biased towards keeping watch for cues of threat, in other words, the child will be hypervigilant, and in a constant state of 'fight, flight or freeze', when not in a dazed state of dorsal shutdown. With only limited ventral vagal activation, this child's neocortex may be underdeveloped, therefore limiting their cognitive development, understanding of language, memory, ability to understand or reflect on their actions and their capacity for empathy.

The attachment behaviours of the infant with a disorganised attachment include the following:

- Moving toward their mother but then moving away from her, or moving towards her while looking away
- Seeking comfort from strangers
- Anxious behaviours which do not involve seeking comfort from others, such as rocking or pulling their own hair
- Appearing to be in a daze – no movements, no response to their name
- Sudden moments of freezing or going into a daze while moving towards their mother.

In the school setting, the child or teenager with a disorganised attachment style might show behaviours such as:

- Having a sense of omnipotence, and not accepting that there are things they don't know
- Constant low-level disruption in lessons
- Trying to control everything
- Not accepting the authority of the teacher (but possibly responding to the head teacher)
- Running out of lessons or running away from school
- Hiding either inside or outside of the school

- Violence toward others or the school
- Inability to sit still or to concentrate, resulting in limited or no academic progress
- Refusing to attempt academic tasks for fear of failure and humiliation
- Putting themselves in risky situations, showing a poor sense of risk
- Showing little to no remorse for actions or empathy for others.

The children and young people at the more extreme end of the disorganised attachment continuum are the most vulnerable we work with and are at high risk of developing mental health issues, involvement with drugs and alcohol, involvement in criminal activity, exploitation, and radicalisation.

It's the day after Keenan's first birthday and he is sitting on the floor in his bedroom with his toys, listening to shouting coming from the floor below. It's a familiar sound. He sits frozen, his whole body tense. There is a loud bang and his body jolts. Keenan isn't yet able to walk, but he can cruise. He crawls to his cot and pulls himself up. He hears another bang. He falls down and lies very still. The door slams opens and his mother storms in, grabbing Keenan's arm and lifting him up, she sits him on her hip and continues shouting at his father, who has followed her in. Keenan starts crying. 'Shut up!' his mother shouts in his face. Keenan freezes again. His father grabs at him, and pulls him away from his mother, who won't let go of his legs. Keenan is crying again. His father has hold of him, but not securely. The man runs down the stairs and into the kitchen, with Keenan screaming under his arm. His mother follows and the argument continues.

Keenan is now 14 and is coming back to school after a 3-day fixed-term exclusion for fighting. He saunters into school, glaring at anyone who makes eye-contact with him. Keenan makes his way to Mrs O'Connor's office, as was the agreement for his first day back. They have a brief chat about the reasons Keenan was excluded, how this was going to be a fresh start, and how Keenan should come to Mrs O'Connor if he is struggling with anything, and especially if he feels like he might start a fight. Keenan agrees. He knows the right things to say. Then he heads off to History. Keenan slams the History classroom door open loudly and throws his bag onto the nearest empty desk. Mr Jones had just started calling the register. 'Morning, Keenan, sit yourself down, please'. 'Yes Sir!' barks Keenan, giving a mock salute, then pulls out his chair, making as much noise as he can. He sits down, rocking backwards on his chair, with his feet on the desk. Mr Jones sighs, 'Keenan, take your feet off the desk and sit sensibly.' Keenan smirks. Mr Jones repeats his request, and Keenan mutters 'Oh f*** off.' 'That's it! Out! Mrs O'Connor's office, NOW!' shouts Mr Jones pointing at the door, as he takes a step towards Keenan. Keenan jumps up, glaring at Mr Jones, then shouts 'Shut up!' in Mr Jones' face before storming out.

Through the Polyvagal Lens ...

Young Keenan had an extremely frightening start to his life. As Keenan's ANS was flooded with cues of threat, his responses ranged from freezing in sympathetic mobilisation, to crying as an attempt at social engagement, to shutting down in the dorsal

> *vagal state. Keenan was in danger. He was not being kept safe by his parents, who left him to play alone in his room at only 12 months old and put him at risk by their dangerous handling of him. Repeated experiences like this will have caused Keenan's ANS to become biased towards detecting cues of threat, while leaving it underdeveloped in its ability to detect cues of safety. Keenan would grow up seeing threat everywhere - even in people simply making eye-contact with him at school. The authority of Mr Jones and possibly the History lesson itself were perceived as threats by Keenan's ANS. He came into that lesson already in sympathetic mobilisation and then remained in that state as he provoked a confrontation with Mr Jones and then fled.*

You may well already have in mind a child or young person you know of who demonstrates some of the attachment behaviours described above. Consider specific incidents of these behaviours and see if you can identify whether the young person was in sympathetic mobilisation or dorsal shutdown, or a blended state of the two. Can you think of any times when this young person seemed to experiencing their ventral vagal state? Possibly not.

Other Ideas about Child Development: Klein and Winnicott

There are several further child development theories that could be considered, but I have chosen to limit our discussion to those that are most relevant in terms of our understanding of emotional wellbeing. However, I do feel we cannot leave the discussion without a mention of Melanie Klein and Donald Winnicott.

The renowned Austrian-British psychoanalyst, Melanie Klein, worked therapeutically with children and progressed our understanding of the child's early psychological development. She emphasised the importance of the baby's relationship with their mother *from birth*, in the development of the child's personality and sense of who they are.

Similarly, Winnicott stressed this point: 'The story of a human being does not start at five years or two, or at six months, but at birth ... and each baby is from the start a person, and needs to be known by someone' (Winnicott, 1964, p. 86).

In his book, *The Child, the Family and the Outside World*, Donald Winnicott describes in detail what effective parenting looks like. He is famous for coining the term 'good enough' parenting, where he suggests that allowing an infant to experience some level of frustration can help build their tolerance of such strong feelings. The mother co-regulates the baby's emotions through secure attachment experiences. As the baby internalises these positive experiences, they start to develop their capacity for self-regulation. In terms of Polyvagal Theory, the baby is repeatedly brought back to their ventral vagal state by their attentive and empathic parent, then given the opportunity to practise this skill for themselves.

Thinking back to 18-month-old Rosie being left at Tina's house, she experienced some difficult feelings when she first realised her mother had gone. For a few moments, she was a little overwhelmed by her feelings of separation anxiety but was then co-regulated by Tina. From experiences such as these, Rosie learnt that she could have these difficult feelings but that they were manageable and would pass. Her tolerance to difficult feelings developed, in turn, building her resilience. Later when starting a new school, she was able to tolerate her anxiety and regulate it, showing she had developed a good level of resilience.

Pulling the Ideas Together

All these theories and ideas have one common thread: *connection*. There are two kinds of connection highlighted in these theories, which support the ideas in Polyvagal Theory.

- Piaget emphasises the connection between the brain and the body as the first stage of development, in other words, the development of the central nervous system.
- Erikson, Vygotsky, Bowlby, Klein and Winnicott all stress the importance of connections with others, that is, the development of the social engagement system.

Through these connections, the developing infant gains an understanding of who they are, what the world is like and their place in the world.

After reading the heart-breaking stories of infants who start their lives with fear and neglect, it might seem that the situation is hopeless for these children and young people, but there are things we, as the influential adults in their lives, can do to help. In later chapters we will explore approaches and activities to help children and young people strengthen their ventral vagal states and develop their capacity to self-regulate, using our understanding of Polyvagal Theory and the child development theories described here.

The human brain and nervous system are not fixed in their function and structure and can be altered through further experiences. This ability of the brain to change in response to stimuli is known as **neuroplasticity**. Bonnie Badenoch explains, 'The foundation for the hope of healing lies in the brain's ability to modify wired-in painful or frightening experiences by activity both within the mind and between minds' (2008, p. 11).

Later we will explore a detailed approach to help the children and young people who have experienced more severe disruptions to their early development. I call this approach the **Connection Diet** (see Chapter 8). These children often have a poor sense of who they are or strong feelings of shame about who they are, difficulty connecting with others and difficulty understanding their own emotional world. Luckily, due to the neuroplasticity of the brain and ANS, changes can be made through repeated positive experiences of connection.

Summary

Learning Points

- The first Piagetian stage (Sensorimotor Stage) of development emphasises the impact of sensory experience on the infant's understanding of the world.
- Erikson highlighted the need for trust in his first stage in child development, leading to autonomy, initiative, industry, and identity.
- Vygotsky connected cognitive development (and therefore learning) with social interactions.
- John Bowlby's Attachment Theory states that the infant develops an attachment style according to the quality of the secure base provided by their attachment figure, and develops attachment behaviours in response to their attachment style.

- The secure attachment style comes from an early experience of sensitive empathic responses from the mother, meeting the infants physical and emotional needs: the infant is co-regulated, and develops their own capacity for self-regulation, thereby developing their ability to bring themselves back to their ventral vagal state after an upset.
- The insecure ambivalent attachment style comes from the infant's experience of a mother who is not sensitive to their needs but is intrusive in their response to the infant. The infant is not co-regulated, therefore develops limited capacity for self-regulation, and experiences high levels of anxiety. The child spends little time in their ventral vagal state and is predominantly in sympathetic mobilisation. Their attachment behaviours are centred around anxiety and control.
- The insecure avoidant attachment style comes from the infant being rejected by the mother, so the infant's physical and/or emotional needs are not met. The infant is not co-regulated and develops limited capacity for self-regulation, which can result in them disconnecting from their overwhelming emotions. The child spends little time in their ventral vagal state and may experience a blended state of sympathetic mobilisation and dorsal shutdown. Their attachment behaviours are centred around independence and isolation.
- The insecure disorganised attachment style is the most worrying of attachment patterns, which comes about from unpredictable and often abusive parenting. The infant's needs are not met, and they are often in a state of terror, leading to sympathetic mobilisation and complete dorsal shutdown. This child will have little or no experience of their ventral vagal state. The attachment behaviours are centred around escaping from threat, which is perceived to be everywhere.
- Neuroplasticity is the ability of the brain and nervous system to change in response to new experiences.
- Connection is the key to healthy child development.

Practical Exercise

Throughout this chapter, I have suggested some short exercises in reflecting on the pupils you work with. Consider now the pupils you have identified in these exercises, and think about strategies you have used so far. What has worked? What has not worked? Reflect on the approaches you have tried in the light of your understanding of child development and Polyvagal Theory. Can you explain *why* your successful strategies have worked?

3 Polyvagal Theory and Childhood Trauma

> We have already explored the effects of insecure attachments and touched on the impact of abusive parenting in Chapter 2. Here we will look in more detail at the effects of **trauma** and abuse on the development of the child's brain and nervous system, specifically the impact on the child's **autonomic nervous system** (ANS). There will also be an overview of the role of hormones.

Defining Trauma

Clinicians and mental health professionals use the American Psychiatric Association's *Diagnostic and Statistical Manual of Mental Disorders* (DSM-5-TR) or the World Health Organization's *International Statistical Classification of Diseases* (ICD-11) as their guide to defining and diagnosing mental health conditions. Trauma is defined by these manuals as: "actual or threatened death, serious injury, or sexual violence" (APA, 2013); "an extremely threatening or horrific event or series of events" (WHO, 2019/2021).

The NHS gives a list of examples of situations that a person could find traumatic and could lead to post-traumatic stress disorder (PTSD):

> serious accidents; physical or sexual assault; abuse, including childhood or domestic abuse; exposure to traumatic events at work, including remote exposure; serious health problems, such as being admitted to intensive care; childbirth experiences, such as losing a baby; the death of someone close to you; war and conflict; torture.
>
> (NHS, 2022)

The word 'serious' appears a few times in these definitions, emphasising the gravity of the experience. I think it can be agreed that a traumatic event is something which is beyond the range of normal life experience and causes a significant level of distress. The term 'threat' is used by the DSM-5 and ICD-11, indicating that the event does not have to cause actual physical harm for it be experienced as traumatic. However, the psychological harm caused by a trauma can lead to physical harm in the form of damage to the nervous system.

DOI: 10.4324/9781003396574-5

We know from **Polyvagal Theory**, that for the autonomic nervous system, a real or perceived threat causes activation of **sympathetic mobilisation** ready for fight, flight, or freeze, followed by **dorsal shutdown** if mobilisation is ineffective against the threat. An experience which is so extreme in terms of its degree of threat causes an extreme response from the ANS, far beyond the responses we encounter on a day-to-day basis. At the time of the trauma, the **neocortex** switches off as the ANS completely hijacks all brain activity, behaviours and body reactions, with survival as its sole objective. With the neocortex out of action, there is no conscious 'thinking' at this time, no processing of what is happening and therefore no real cognitive understanding.

A traumatic event can overload the ANS, causing changes in the function and structure of the nervous system. Remember **neuroplasticity** enables a reshaping of the nervous system due to new experiences. If the new experience involves overwhelming psychological distress, the nervous system adapts to the new understanding of a terrifying and dangerous world. The ANS becomes biased towards scanning for cues of threat and the traumatised person can remain stuck in sympathetic mobilisation or dorsal shutdown, or both. Peter Levine describes what life is like for traumatised people, "They are unable to overcome the anxiety of their experience. They remain overwhelmed by the event, defeated and terrified. Virtually imprisoned by their fear, they are unable to re-engage with life" (1997, p. 28).

Meanwhile, the memory of the trauma cannot be processed like normal memories as the neocortex was offline at the time of the trauma. The emotional intensity is beyond what the limbic system can cope with, so the memory becomes trapped within the limbic system, constantly being replayed. "The trauma may be over, but it keeps being replayed in continually recycling memories and in a reorganised nervous system" (Van Der Kolk, 2014, p. 157).

Considering these extensive effects of a traumatic event on the life of an adult, what further impact does it have on the mind and nervous system of the developing child?

Early Trauma and Brain Development

You should be familiar with forms of child abuse from your child protection training, but I will give an overview here, along with other experiences that are not abuse but could be traumatic. It is important that we appreciate the breadth of experiences which are traumatic to the developing child.

As mentioned above, traumatic experiences include physical violence and sexual violence. For children who experience such trauma, there is also a devastating impact on their development.

I would urge you to revisit your child protection training if you feel unfamiliar with any of the examples given in the list below and ensure that you are fully aware of your establishment's safeguarding policy, including the actions you should take if you have any concerns about the safety of a child. All the following are forms of abuse and can be classed as traumatic:

- Physical abuse
- Sexual abuse, including non-contact and online sexual abuse

- Grooming
- Child sexual exploitation
- Peer-on-peer abuse and bullying
- Online abuse, including cyberbullying
- Criminal exploitation, gangs and 'county lines'
- Child trafficking
- Female genital mutilation
- Neglect
- Emotional abuse, including exposing the child to distressing experiences.

Traumas experienced before adulthood are sometimes known as **adverse childhood experiences (ACEs)** and can include living with a person with serious mental illness, having a parent who is in prison, or having a parent addicted to drugs or alcohol. A study conducted in England in 2016 found just under 45 per cent of adults have experienced at least one ACE (Ford et al., 2016). We know that reports of childhood abuse in the home increased during the pandemic lockdowns. I can't help but wonder what impact the pandemic will have had on the prevalence of ACEs and the long-term effects on the mental health of today's children.

For a young child, their survival depends on adults meeting their needs, so any threat to these needs being met could also be experienced as traumatic. Further to the list of forms of abuse and the ACEs, abandonment, rejection, loss, or witnessing a parent being threatened or harmed are all traumatic to the helpless infant. As explored in Chapter 2, neglect of a child's attachment needs can have detrimental effects on the development of the child's ANS. This can be extended to all forms of emotional abuse.

The infant who grows up with repeated threats to their survival, will experience repeated activation of their survival responses, i.e., sympathetic mobilisation and/or dorsal shutdown. As we know, the neocortex deactivates at these times of threat, so its development for this infant will be disrupted. The child may therefore have underdeveloped cognitive functioning, including poor understanding and use of language, limited capacity for learning and problem solving, and a poor sense of empathy. Meanwhile, the parts of their brain which have been taking control will become overdeveloped. The brain of this child adapts to the environment they are growing in. The child's nervous system learns to constantly scan for signs of threat and always be ready for action. This child is always in 'survival mode', and their brain and ANS have developed for optimum functioning in their dangerous world.

Of course, this child then starts school, expecting to find danger. With an ANS so inexperienced in recognising signs of safety, the child is likely to misread people and situations as threatening. The lack of familiarity could be felt as a threat. People making eye-contact could be a threat. An unexpected sound could be a threat. A strange smell could be a threat. Explaining to this child that they are safe will be ineffective because they are not in their ventral vagal state. Therefore, their neocortex is offline, along with their social engagement system and they cannot easily understand language. This is a very challenging situation for the staff trying to manage the child's fight, flight, freeze and/or shutdown behaviours.

Kyle started living with his current foster carers when he was 6, after two placement breakdowns. At the age of 4, Kyle was found wandering the streets near his home alone at night. During those first few years of his life, he was rarely fed enough food, ignored by his mother, and as soon as he could walk, he was shut out of the house for hours at a time. His first two foster placements broke down due to Kyle's challenging behaviours of running away from home, violence towards his foster carers and constantly stealing.

Kyle is now 11 years old and has been settled with his current foster carers for a few years. He has an EHCP due to his emotional and social difficulties, and some learning needs. Before the start of Y7, he spent a little time with the SENCo and with Miss Kinsella, the LSA who would be supporting him in most of his lessons. It's the second week of Y7, and Kyle is in a science lesson, with Miss Kinsella sitting next to him. The teacher is giving instructions for the experiment they are about to conduct. Kyle isn't listening to the teacher, and instead is telling Miss Kinsella he wants her pen. The teacher asks Kyle to pay attention to the instructions. Kyle snatches Miss Kinsella's pen from her hand and throws it at the teacher. He then runs out of the room.

Through the Polyvagal Lens …

Kyle's most basic survival needs of shelter, food and safety were not met when he was an infant, so his early brain development would have been disrupted as his ANS would have been keeping him in 'survival mode' most of the time. He would likely have been in sympathetic mobilisation when out alone at night. He may have learnt to steal food, to run away from dangers, to do anything he needed to keep himself safe. His ANS would have become highly effective at watching for cues of threat, but unfamiliar with cues of safety. Kyle would have learnt that adults are not a source of comfort or protection. Meanwhile, Kyle's learning of language, development of empathy, his ability to play and be creative, and his social development would all have been severely disrupted. In Kyle's case, an EHCP was in place to address some of these needs.

In the science lesson, Kyle felt a need to have Miss Kinsella's pen, and hadn't developed strategies to manage the overwhelming feeling of this unmet need. His ANS would have read the situation of having his need not being met as a threat, quickly erupting into sympathetic mobilisation (fight then flight) when the teacher, another potential threat, spoke to him.

Later we will explore approaches to working with a child in this state. There is no quick fix, but thanks to **neuroplasticity**, work can be done to help reshape the child's nervous system, so their ANS can identify cues of safety. We can strengthen their **ventral vagal state**, address the disrupted development of their **neocortex**, develop more secure attachments and help them see a new safer world.

The Biased ANS

In Chapter 1, we were introduced to the idea that cues of safety and threat can be classified as *internal*, *external*, or *relational*. Here we will explore this idea further.

Internal Cues

As you are reading, you may be aware of how your body is feeling. Whether you feel hot, cold or comfortable, whether you feel hungry, or need the toilet, or have a headache, etc. These are all common examples of *internal* feedback from your body. Other examples which might not have such an obvious cause include your heartrate increasing slightly, tension in certain muscles in your body, goosebumps when it's not cold, yawning when you're not tired, a warm feeling inside when you see/hear something beautiful. These and many others are all internal cues of safety and cues of threat detected by your ANS. A pain in your body is an obvious cue of threat. It distracts you from what you're doing and causes you to consciously respond. It may raise your heartrate and breathing rate as your sympathetic nervous system is activated. With your ventral vagal system still online, and therefore your social engagement system active, you may seek comfort from someone close to you – a strategy you will have learnt from childhood as a means of emotional regulation.

For the traumatised person, this may be a very different experience. First, trauma can cause a child to have a very limited connection to their body. Some abused children cannot tell when they need the toilet, whether they are hot or cold, when they are full from eating, and they may even not notice a pain in their body. Other traumatised children read every internal cue as a sign of threat and are constantly distracted by body sensations, sending them into sympathetic mobilisation and/or dorsal shutdown.

Noah experienced physical abuse as an infant. His mother frequently hit him and kicked him when she became angry. As a toddler his heart raced when he heard her start shouting and he would run to his hiding place in the cupboard under the stairs, where he would make himself small and stay very still and quiet.

Now 6 years old, Noah is at school playing football outside at lunchtime. The ball is coming towards him, and he stands a chance of scoring a goal. His teammates start shouting his name in excitement. Noah feels his heart racing and starts running but runs straight past the ball to the edge of the playground, where he quickly curls up small behind a tree.

Through the Polyvagal Lens ...

Noah's early experience of physical danger caused his ANS to become biased towards searching for cues of threat. The internal cue of his heart racing became a cue of threat as it was associated with danger. People shouting, feeling his raised heartrate and then running all took Noah back to his earlier experiences. His ANS took over and sent him into complete sympathetic mobilisation as he ran away and hid. There was no conscious thought involved in this response and, if questioned afterwards, Noah would not have been able to explain why he acted as he did.

How often is it the case that a child is questioned about their actions or behaviours, and they seem to have no coherent explanation?

External Cues

Your ANS is constantly scanning your body for internal cues of safety and threat, but also your environment. The smell of smoke, a loud unexpected bang, a car about to drive into you – all external cues of threat. Then there's the sound of your favourite song, a scent that brings back a treasured memory, having a soothing hot bath – external cues of safety. Examples of cues of safety are varied and personal. In Chapter 5 we will explore this in more detail as you get to know your own ANS.

Sometimes for the traumatised children we work with, the cue of threat that they are responding to can be extremely difficult to identify. As the ANS takes control of the child's behaviours, the child is unlikely to know what the cue of threat is either. For instance, you may find you are faced with challenging protection-driven behaviours from the child, such as fighting or running away, because you happen to have a similar scent to the adult who harmed the child. The child may be sent into sympathetic mobilisation and/or dorsal shutdown by certain noises, by the room being too bright or too dark, by sudden movements.

From the age of 4 to 7 years old, Megan was sexually abused by her step-dad. He always clicked the end of his pen as he was looking at his phone moments before he would turn to Megan then take her by the arm upstairs.

Megan is now in Year 9. Her step-dad is in prison and she has had counselling to help her process her experience. Megan is doing well in school and enjoys her lessons. She is in her Maths lesson with Mrs Bennett. The class are working through some problems quietly and Mrs Bennett is quietly walking around checking how her pupils are doing. Megan is concentrating on her work and making good progress through the questions. Mrs Bennett is holding her new pen and clicking the end absent-mindedly as she walks. She stops at Megan's desk as she notices that Megan is staring ahead blankly. She gently says Megan's name but gets no response. She puts her hand on Megan's shoulder and says her name again. After a few minutes Megan suddenly looks at Mrs Bennett, then starts shaking. She tearfully asks Mrs Bennett what happened.

Through the Polyvagal Lens ...

Megan's ANS learnt that the clicking sound was an external sign of threat. During the abuse, it is likely that Megan's ANS took her into dorsal shutdown as sympathetic mobilisation would have been ineffective in keeping her safe. Despite Megan <u>being</u> safe and <u>feeling</u> safe in her maths lesson, the clicking was such a strong cue of threat that her ANS immediately took over and sent her into dorsal shutdown. As she came out of this state, she moved through sympathetic mobilisation on the way back to her ventral vagal state, hence the shaking. Mrs Bennett provided cues of safety and activated Megan's social engagement system, both helping Megan return to her ventral vagal state.

Relational Cues

These are cues of threat and safety from interactions with other people. As stated in Chapter 1, your ANS talks to the ANS of every person you interact with. If your ANS is detecting cues of threat, it will be communicating this threat to others *on an unconscious level*. Have you ever been in a situation where you have looked at someone and within seconds you knew something was wrong? We detect relational cues of threat and safety through subtle changes in body language, tone of voice, facial expressions. As discussed in Chapter 1, you may have had the experience of being able to tell if someone's smile is genuine or fake, due to the nuances detected by your ANS.

Tanesha was brought to the UK when she was 5 years old by a stranger who she was told was her aunt. Tanesha's mother had reassured her that she would be joining Tanesha next week in their new home. Tanesha's mother had cared well for her daughter and truly believed they would be reunited. Once in London, Tanesha was taken to a house where seven other children lived with a woman called Auntie Grace. Tanesha asked about her mother. Auntie Grace smiled wryly at Tanesha and said her mother didn't want her any more.

Tanesha was made to clean the house and as she got older, she took care of the younger children. If Tanesha didn't do as Auntie Grace told her, she would be beaten.

It wasn't until Tanesha was 8 years old that Social Services discovered the situation, and the children were taken into care. Tanesha has now started attending school. She is often taken out of her class for 1:1 lessons with Mrs Lloyd to address the gaps in her learning. Initially Tanesha doesn't make eye-contact with Mrs Lloyd, and rarely speaks. Mrs Lloyd always sits a little way from Tanesha, to give her space and speaks in a gentle voice. She frequently smiles warmly at Tanesha, even when Tanesha isn't looking at her. After a few weeks, Tanesha risks looking at Mrs Lloyd and then nervously starts to speak to her.

Through the Polyvagal Lens ...

Tanesha's ANS would have become more biased towards detecting cues of threat during her traumatic three years with Auntie Grace, leaving her less able to trust any cues of safety. Tanesha had good parenting from her mother until she was taken away at age 5, resulting in healthy development of her brain and nervous system up to this point. Mrs Lloyd had a strong ventral vagal state and used her ANS to communicate messages of safety to Tanesha's ANS. The repeated experience of relational cues of safety from Mrs Lloyd started bringing Tanesha back to her ventral vagal state, also bringing her social engagement system back online.

Notice that both Auntie Grace and Mrs Lloyd smiled at Tanesha but were conveying very different messages.

Lisa Dion (2018) suggests that threats can be sorted into four categories: physical pain; the unknown; incongruence; unrealistic expectations and 'shoulds'.

We have considered the first of these categories, *physical pain*, in the *internal* cues of threat. The second category, *the unknown*, is widely accepted as a common human fear. The fear itself is more about what danger there might be, not about cues of actual threat. For instance, a fear of the dark is about what danger might be lurking in the dark, rather than the actual absence of light. Darkness itself does not pose a threat. For the traumatised child, this fear of what might be can feel all too real, as they have first-hand experience of the potential danger.

Incongruence was explored in Chapter 1, where we looked at the idea of adults attempting to fake feeling calm when their ANS is sending signals that things are in fact not OK. If Mrs Lloyd was not in her ventral vagal state, her body language, tone of voice and facial expressions would have indicated so and Tanesha would not have felt any safer.

Unrealistic expectations and messages that we 'should' act like this, we 'shouldn't' feel like that, etc., are all threats to our sense of who we are. When expectations put on us are unmet and we don't fit the 'shoulds', we are left with the dilemma over who we really are and who we think we should be, and at risk of denying our authentic self. This threat to our sense of self can cause activation of our defence systems. For the developing child, their sense of who they are is still forming, so they are more vulnerable to these messages, and to this dilemma.

Hormones

To give a fuller picture of what happens in the developing child's body in response to trauma, I feel it is worth mentioning our chemical messengers: hormones.

There are many hormones at work in your body at this very moment, controlling various processes, such as digestion, metabolism, blood pressure, blood sugar levels. We will explore just a few that play an important role in the body reactions to stress.

- *Cortisol - the stress hormone*: Made by the adrenal gland, cortisol helps regulate metabolism, blood sugar levels, blood pressure and reduce inflammation. At times of stress, as part of the sympathetic mobilisation response, cortisol increases heart rate, muscle tension and metabolism, and shuts down digestion and reproduction processes. After the stressful situation has passed, cortisol returns to its baseline level, however, after a traumatic event, it can remain at a high level, keeping the body in a continuous state of sympathetic mobilisation (Van der Kolk, 2014).
- *Serotonin - the mood stabiliser*: A chemical found throughout the body, serotonin has a role in regulating anxiety and sleep, healing wounds and bowel movements. Low levels of serotonin in the brain are linked to depression. Stress in infancy can cause a reduction in serotonin levels later in life (Gerhardt, 2015).
- *Oxytocin - the love hormone*: Found in the brain, oxytocin has a role in social interactions and attachment. Oxytocin levels rise with physical contact with another person, and at childbirth. An insecure attachment very early in an infant's life can result in a lack of oxytocin, which can lead to a poorly regulated fear response (ibid.).
- *Dopamine - the reward hormone*: A chemical found in the brain, dopamine acts as a 'reward centre', and is involved with memory, movement, motivation, attention and learning. Poor interactions in infancy, such as those in the insecure attachments we explored in Chapter 2, lead to low levels of dopamine (ibid.).

For the infant who is born into a safe nurturing environment with a secure attachment, cortisol levels are regulated through the **co-regulation** from their mother, and the helpful hormones of serotonin, oxytocin and dopamine are set at optimum baselines for the healthy growth and development of the child. Early experiences of trauma can cause unregulated levels of these hormones, the baselines to be set too high or too low, or for the hormone levels to increase or decrease in an unpredictable uncontrolled manner. Children such as Kyle and Noah, whom we met earlier, are likely to have high cortisol levels due to high activation of their sympathetic mobilisation systems.

When we consider the more challenging behaviours of the children we work with, it is worth holding in mind that not only may their brain and nervous system development have been ruptured by trauma, but also their hormone levels.

Connection - Protection

To simplify the way we look at behaviours, it can be useful to think of them as on a continuum, with Connection at one end and Protection at the other.

Connection ←---→ **Protection**

In your ventral vagal state, your **social engagement system** is online, and you are at the Connection end of the spectrum. When your ANS detects a threat, you start moving towards the Protection end. Initially you might seek support from another person (connection) but as you experience some sympathetic mobilisation (protection), you move further away from connecting with others and move into protective behaviours such as escaping from the situation, preparing to fight, or shutting down. If the states of sympathetic mobilisation or dorsal shutdown take over, and your ventral vagal state is switched off, you have moved completely to the Protection end of the spectrum and your behaviours may include isolating yourself from others and feeling disconnected from your body, i.e., breaking connections.

This can be a very useful model for thinking about the behaviours of children and young people. Think back to some of the youngsters we have met so far. Where on the continuum would you place Noah *while* he was playing football, and *then* when he ran away and hid? Where was Megan when Mrs Bennett first said her name? Consider now some of the challenging behaviours of children or young people you have worked with. Was the behaviour closer to Connection or Protection? When we think of the stories of Kyle, Noah or Megan, although we are only given a snapshot of their experiences, we can clearly see where their behaviours have come from. We have very little, if any, idea of exactly what the children in our care have experienced, so we cannot as easily see how their behaviours connect with their past. What we can do is acknowledge how much we don't know and focus on what the current behaviours are telling us. Some children, especially those who have been traumatised, spend most of their time down the Protection end of the scale. We can help them find their way to the Connection end, in other words strengthen their ventral vagal state, using activities such as those in the 'Connection Diet', described in Part II.

Sadie was groomed by her uncle from infancy, and sexually abused by him until she was 6, when her mother found out. Sadie disclosed that the abuse had happened at her uncle's house next door, on most days.

Now 9 years old, Sadie is sitting with her friends in the school hall, eating lunch. She eats everything she is given and accepts offers of her friends' leftovers. Sadie often eats more than everyone else. Today she has eaten more than usual, but doesn't stop eating. As they get up, to head outside, Sadie is sick on the floor. The Midday Assistant comes to Sadie's aid, taking her to the First Aider, Mrs Gibbs, in the front office. Sadie frequently visits Mrs Gibbs, as she has vomited at lunchtime on several occasions. She also visits Mrs Gibbs when she wets herself in the classroom, which happens at least once a week. Mrs Gibbs smiles and asks Sadie if she ate too much again. Sadie shrugs. Mrs Gibbs reminds her of the rule that she only needs to eat what is on her plate, whilst Sadie sits quietly with a small cup of water. Mrs Gibbs then makes sure that Sadie goes to the toilet, before sending her out to play.

Through the Polyvagal Lens ...

Sadie's early repeated experience of her body being violated, sending her into complete dorsal shutdown, weakened the connection between her mind and her body. Her ANS, as an attempt to protect her from the impact of the abuse, broke the connection with her body sensations. Sadie was left unable to recognise messages from her body, such as those saying she was full or that she needed the toilet. Her ANS had kept her at the Protection end of the continuum.

Summary

Learning Points

- Trauma can be thought of as an experience beyond the range of normal human life experiences, which causes significant distress. During a traumatic event, memories are not processed in the normal way.
- An infant's developing brain adapts to its environment; therefore an abusive childhood can result in underdeveloped higher thinking (in the neocortex) and overdeveloped survival behaviours.
- An abused child may develop a biased ANS, which is adapted to detecting unconscious cues of threat, but is unfamiliar with unconscious cues of safety.
- Cues of threat or safety can be classified as internal (within the body), external (outside of the body) or relational (in interactions with other people).
- Other types of threat include the unknown, incongruence and unrealistic expectations (including 'shoulds').
- Hormones help regulate processes in the body and can become unbalanced by childhood trauma: cortisol - the stress hormone; serotonin - the mood stabiliser; oxytocin - the love hormone; dopamine - the reward hormone.
- Behaviours can be thought of as on a continuum from Connection to Protection.

Practical Exercise

Think of a child whom you suspect or know to have experienced trauma and consider their behaviours. What does their behaviour *communicate* about their ANS? Where would you put this child on the Connection-Protection continuum? What types of perceived threat do you notice them responding to? Have you seen this child behaving in a calm and connected way? If so, what cues of safety can you think of that the child's ANS might have been detecting? Were they external? Relational?

4 Seeing Your Pupils through the Lens of Polyvagal Theory

As a professional working with children or young people in an education setting, you are likely to have encountered the child in the mobilised fight/flight/freeze state, or the child who seems shut down and hard to reach. You will have realised that when a child is in either of these states, they have lost their capacity to learn, and therefore are unable to make the expected academic progress. In this chapter we will look at different ways to view behaviour and explore how **Polyvagal Theory** can help to make sense of what is happening for our pupils. Instead of an exercise at the end of the chapter, there will be detailed exercises in the last two sections.

The Meaning of Behaviour

A child's challenging behaviour can be seen as having two purposes: (1) to meet an unmet need; and (2) to communicate. We have explored the idea of behaviour being on a continuum from Connection to Protection. The more challenging behaviours we see in school tend to be in order to meet the unmet need of protection and communicate to us that the child is not feeling safe. These protection-driven survival behaviours are often a result of the child being hijacked by **sympathetic mobilisation**, with minimal or no ventral vagal activation and therefore limited thinking, reasoning, empathising or connection with others.

Human needs have been explained in the well-known visual representation of **Maslow's Hierarchy of Needs** (Figure 4.1).

This is a useful model in helping us identify the unmet needs that a child's behaviour is attempting to address. We can see that the most basic needs of the human body for survival are at the base: air, water, food, shelter, warmth, etc. Then safety follows quickly as the next level. When a child's behaviour communicates an unmet need, it is worth first considering the very basic needs. Is this child hungry? Tired?

Then consider whether the child feels safe. Remember there could be cues of threat that you are unaware of, and *being* safe does not mean *feeling* safe.

Working our way up Maslow's Hierarchy, the next level is Love and Belonging. Is the child's behaviour telling you that they feel excluded? That they have no friends? It seems that

DOI: 10.4324/9781003396574-6

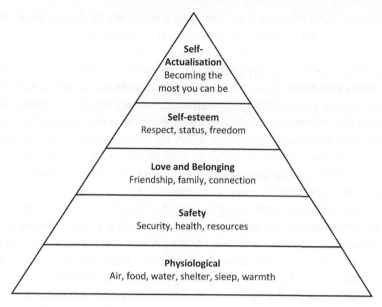

Figure 4.1 Maslow's Hierarchy of Needs

'attention-seeking' has become a common term for describing a child's behaviour, with very negative connotations. I wonder if this is because the behaviours feel like an attempt at manipulation. Understandably, we don't like the feeling of being manipulated. This may be why it is difficult to remain patient with the child or young person showing these behaviours. It is worth considering where these behaviours are coming from. If the child is desperately trying to seek your attention, it is likely that they are not getting the care and attention they need elsewhere. As educator and student mentor, Nicholas Ferroni said, "Students who are loved at home, come to school to learn, and students who aren't, come to school to be loved."

Self-regulation, co-regulation and Dysregulation

Another way of understanding a child's challenging behaviour is as an attempt at **self-regulation**. Children engage in varied and sometimes baffling behaviours as attempts to manage their emotions or sensations. Children naturally wriggle, fidget, roll around on the floor, run, climb, skip, hang upside down, jump, spin, sing ... the list goes on. In primary schools, opportunities to play freely are usually considered an essential part of the timetable. Playgrounds are full of equipment to allow for all the body movements and activities children are naturally drawn to. Children have a strong body-mind connection and follow their body's signals until unfortunately they are taught not to. How many children do you know who find it difficult to sit still in their chair? You might find you are battling with their natural body messages to move. Regular breaks for movement around the room, and/or the use of fidget toys are strategies that can help some, if not most children.

In secondary schools, free time is often undervalued. All too often the pupils with challenging behaviours end up losing their free time to detentions or meetings about their behaviour, when these are the young people who need that time the most. Consider one of the young people you know who lost their lunchtime due to their behaviour. Were they trying to self-regulate with these behaviours? Were they experiencing sympathetic mobilisation?

For some dysregulated children and young people, their body signals are telling them to act in ways that are ineffective at regulation, and therefore keep them in sympathetic mobilisation or **dorsal shutdown**. These behaviours might include hitting, biting, pushing, hiding, avoiding eye-contact, breaking things, swearing, screaming, avoiding speaking, self-harm, avoiding eating and for older children or young people the behaviours could include substance/drug/alcohol abuse, promiscuity, vandalism, arson, etc. These behaviours are failed attempts to self-regulate and are detrimental to the child or young person's wellbeing. As Lisa Dion explains: 'The more time a child spends in the freeze/flight/fight/collapse response, the higher the probability that the child will experience problems in areas such as health, relationship, learning rage and depression, and impulsivity' (2018, p. 51). This is when the child needs our help, through **co-regulation**. The child needs us to lend them our strong **ventral vagal state** through communication from our ANS to theirs. We will look later at specific strategies to help the dysregulated child and develop their ability to self-regulate. For now, it is worth holding onto the idea that their behaviour is a maladaptive strategy to manage overwhelming feelings. These children need **empathy** and understanding, not judgement and punishment.

Impact of the COVID-19 Pandemic

Even though the pandemic happened a few years ago now, we are still feeling the effects, and I believe we will do so for some time to come. As adults, we know that our anxiety levels were significantly impacted. Many suffered bereavements, financial difficulties, physical health problems directly or indirectly as a result of the virus and mental health problems. Alongside anxiety, there was loneliness, depression, anger, hopelessness, helplessness, and despair. Children and young people did not escape the effects of the pandemic, however much their parents might have tried to protect them. Many aspects of the development of our children and young people were impacted, especially social development and learning as schools closed during the lockdowns. The higher anxiety levels in the adults around them and the new unfamiliar daily routine, at the very least, would have affected all children and young people. Many children and young people would have experienced higher anxiety, and increased activation of their sympathetic mobilisation state. Every adult's ANS at that time would have been sending out unconscious messages that there is a threat, and every child's developing ANS would have picked up on this message. Our resilience, our capacity for self-regulation, the strength of everyone's ventral vagal state - they were all being tested by the threat of COVID-19.

Life has now returned to 'normal', although for many people, this is not their pre-pandemic normal. Loss of loved ones, financial hardship, ongoing mental health difficulties, 'long COVID' and other ongoing challenges are still taking their toll. For children and young people, their development now has the task of recovering from the disruption. I have heard from many teaching professionals that young people are not showing the social maturity expected for their age. There are still gaps in learning that are being addressed, and there are signs of lower resilience and higher anxiety in children and young people of all ages.

Anxiety can present itself in many ways in children and young people. It is an emotional state associated with sympathetic mobilisation, and therefore tends to be seen in behaviours involving movement and tension, rather than shutdown.

For children, they might show their anxiety through:

* Sleeping difficulties, and/or nightmares
* Eating problems, for instance, only eating certain foods
* Increased sensory issues
* Somatised responses, e.g., headaches or stomach ache
* Crying more than usual
* Defiance
* Being easily distracted and unable to focus
* Panic attacks
* Trying to control everything
* Tantrums
* Avoiding places or situations, e.g., refusing to go to school
* Constant worrying
* Putting high expectations on themselves
* Angry outbursts
* Insisting on following routines or rituals

Seven-year-old Ellie is supposed to be getting dressed for school, but her favourite tights are in the wash and her mum has asked her to put socks on instead. Ellie knows she doesn't like the feel of her socks, and she thought she would be wearing her tights today. She starts breathing fast and begins to cry, as she picks up the socks, then drops them on the floor. She then sits on the floor, sobbing. Her mum comes in, helps Ellie up and sits her on the edge of the bed. She asks what's wrong, but Ellie doesn't answer. Her mum realises it's the tights problem again, and exasperated, she fishes yesterday's tights out of the wash basket. 'Here, put these on!' she snaps, then leaves the room. Ellie, still crying, shouts, 'I'm not going!' and throws the tights across the room. She kicks at her bedroom door, repeatedly shouting 'I hate you!' for the next half hour. Ellie doesn't make it to school that day.

Through the Polyvagal Lens …

Ellie's reaction to not having her tights to wear is extreme. There are two issues raising Ellie's anxiety to overwhelming levels – the sensory feeling of the socks, which is something she knows she doesn't like, and the unexpected change to what she thought was going to happen. For a child whose anxiety level is already high, small issues such as these can overwhelm them. The ANS is on the lookout for anything amiss, and the ventral vagal state is fragile, with sympathetic mobilisation ready for activation at the smallest provocation. This child is likely to be in a blended state of ventral vagal and sympathetic mobilisation much of the time. For Ellie, her ANS quickly activated her sympathetic mobilisation system as her breathing rate increased and she started crying. Ellie's strong unconscious cues of threat from her ANS were detected by her mum's ANS, as her sympathetic mobilisation was also activated, hence the snapping at Ellie (fight) and leaving the room (flight).

Older children or teenagers might show anxiety through any of the above, but might also:

- Self-harm
- Use alcohol or drugs to reduce their anxiety
- Develop inflexible compulsive behaviours, which could be focused on exercise, school work, eating, gaming, sports, social media
- Express suicidal thoughts
- Express disordered thoughts, such as delusional thinking, confusion or auditory, visual or tactile hallucinations

---

Ali is in sixth form college, studying A-Levels, with plans to go to uni next year to study Law. He was predicted to get high grades but did not do as well in his mocks as hoped. Ali did not sit his GCSE exams as it was the year of pandemic lockdowns and school closures. His A-Level exams will be his first experience of public exams. Every evening, Ali plays an online game, on the PC in his room. It started as an hour or so, after online lessons during the pandemic, and he found it a nice way to 'spend time' with his mates. Now he plays five or more hours as soon as he gets home, and he doesn't know the people he's playing with. His friends lost interest in the game some time ago. Ali's mum has noticed that he often looks tired and doesn't go out with his friends like he used to before COVID. She also suspects he's been missing lessons and coming home early. She has tried talking to Ali about her concerns, but when she does, he blanks her and heads straight for his room. She discovered recently that he has put a lock on his bedroom door.

Through the Polyvagal Lens ...

Ali's anxiety was relieved a little during the pandemic with an activity that activated his social engagement system, thereby strengthening his ventral vagal state. He couldn't spend time with his friends in person, but gaming was the next best thing. However, his anxiety level from this time remained high, and the academic pressures were too high for him to cope with. His survival response led him into a compulsion to play the online game, despite his friends having left the game. The game provided as escape (flight) from the overwhelming anxiety of college. With a weaker ventral vagal state, Ali's social engagement system was less active, resulting in fewer actual social interactions, such as spending time with his mum or going out with his friends. Ali was likely in blended state of sympathetic mobilisation and dorsal shutdown.

Consider the young people or children you work with. Have you seen an increase in any of the behaviours listed since the pandemic? With the young people and children I have worked with myself, I have noticed that, for some, the symptoms of their anxiety are only coming to light now, a few years after the pandemic.

In Part II, in Chapter 8, we will explore exercises to increase resilience, help young people recognise anxiety and present strategies for managing anxiety.

Keep in mind the range of behaviours that could indicate anxiety, and that the fallout from the pandemic could be felt for some time to come, especially for children and young people whose development was impacted.

Neurodevelopmental Conditions

Anxiety is known well to many people who are autistic. You may recognise some of the anxiety-driven behaviours listed above as those of pupils you know to have a diagnosis of **autism**. Unfortunately, these behaviours are sometimes simply labelled as autistic behaviours and the accompanying anxiety is overlooked.

For the dysregulated autistic child, co-regulation can be achieved using the same fundamental idea suggested for co-regulating any dysregulated child: that your ANS is talking to their ANS, therefore, if you are in a strong ventral vagal state, your ANS will send cues of safety and help them return to their ventral vagal state. A colleague of mine told me of an experience she had calming an autistic teenage boy in an alternative education provision, which demonstrates this point well.

PJ was a 16-year-old boy with a big build. He had a history of violence towards adults when he was distressed, which easily happened when things were not following the plan he had been told. For this reason, staff were generally wary of him. My colleague was in the classroom next door to where PJ was and she could hear him talking loudly, clearly becoming distressed. She went to investigate. She stopped at the doorway to the classroom to briefly observe the situation. Two staff members were standing on the other side of the small classroom from PJ, behind a table, looking anxious, trying to respond to what he was saying. PJ was sitting at the desk frowning and speaking loudly and becoming aggressive in his tone. My colleague knew of PJ's history and had met him but had not yet established a relationship with him. She walked confidently but calmly into the room and sat at the desk a little way from PJ. She said to him that she could see something had upset him and asked if he could tell her about it. PJ explained his grievance to her in a quieter voice and his aggression subsided, as she listened. The two other staff members then joined them at the desk.

Through the Polyvagal Lens ...

Before you read the explanation below, take a moment to see if you can explain what happened yourself, using what you have learnt about Polyvagal Theory.

My colleague told me that she had been feeling confident in herself and didn't feel threatened by PJ, so she didn't feel that it was an unreasonable risk to sit near him. Her ANS would have been sending PJ's ANS cues of safety, which he was not receiving from the two anxious staff members on the other side of the room. They had been feeling threatened and their sympathetic mobilisation had started taking over, sending them to the other side of the room in a state of fight/flight/freeze. Their ANS would have been sending PJ's ANS cues of threat, causing him to also move into sympathetic mobilisation. The situation was escalating as unconscious cues of threat were being sent back and forth. My colleague had a strong ventral vagal state as she co-regulated all three of them. Her words were not so different from what the other staff members had been saying, it was her unconscious communication (from her ANS) that made the difference.

When working with autistic children, even those who are non-communicative, it is the strength of your ventral vagal state and therefore the strength of your unconscious cues of safety that will help you co-regulate the child. This is the case for children with any **neuro-developmental condition**. Difficulties with communication, learning new information, tics, processing sensory input, social skills, recall, movement, etc. do not impair the communication between your ANS and theirs. Some of the activities suggested in Part II may be unsuitable for some children with special educational needs (SEND), but they could be adapted, and the fundamental idea that your ANS is constantly talking to the ANS of the child will always hold true.

Tracking Autonomic States

Consider now the class or group of children you work most closely with. There may be some with special needs or known early **trauma** which you can keep in mind when thinking about their behaviours. Think of the last lesson you had with this class and note down your answers to these questions:

1. At the start of the lesson, what was the atmosphere in the class? Think of three words you would use to describe how the class felt. Looking at the words you have chosen, decide where you would put them on the Connection-Protection scale.

   Connection ←---→ **Protection**

   For example, you might think of words such as noisy, focused, jumbled, interested, fussy, hostile, playful, jumpy, chaotic, sleepy, excitable, irritable, flat, tearful.
   Your words might be at different places on the scale, possibly indicating very separate groups within the class, or they may be all together.
2. Think of any key moments in the lesson, such as a change in activity. Think of three words to describe how the lesson felt in these moments, and decide where the class was on the scale.
3. Which three words would you choose to describe the feeling in the classroom at the end of the lesson? Where on the scale was the class now?
4. Consider now whether there were particular pupils who made more of a contribution than others to the atmosphere of the class. Where was each of these pupils on the scale at the beginning, during and the end of the lesson?
5. If you had a child heading towards the protection end of the scale, they would be moving through sympathetic mobilisation before reaching dorsal shutdown. What specific behaviours tell you they were experiencing sympathetic mobilisation (fight/flight/freeze)?
6. Which children were in their ventral vagal state for most of the lesson? How could you tell?

Recognising and tracking where the children, and the class as a whole, are in terms of their **autonomic states** give us insight into their experience of our lessons and guide us on how to help strengthen their ventral vagal states. It helps us learn to spot the early signs of sympathetic mobilisation and dorsal shutdown and use our own ANS to change the atmosphere of the classroom, like my colleague earlier with PJ.

Which words would you *like* to choose to describe the atmosphere in your lessons? Hopefully these would be words you'd associate with the ventral vagal state, and you'd place them at the Connection end of the scale.

Renaming the Autonomic States

Sometimes the words we choose can really help bring this idea of tracking the autonomic states to life. Think of a particular child you work with and you feel you know reasonably well. We are going to consider ways of labelling this child's autonomic states using more descriptive terms, which will feel like they really fit for this child.

- *Ventral vagal state* - When this child is feeling connected to you, to their peers, to themselves, and is at their best for learning. Which words would you use to describe them? For example, chilled, focused, settled, interested, curious, funny...
- *Sympathetic mobilisation* - It may be that the child is in a **blended state** (such as sympathetic *and* ventral), but their sympathetic mobilisation may cause them to be on edge or anxious. Remember this is the state that causes tension in the body, and the **neocortex** (higher thinking) is not working as efficiently. How would you describe them in this state? For example, fidgety, distracted, squirmy, chatty, forgetful, sarcastic, jumpy...
- *Dorsal shutdown* - Again, the child might be in a blended state, but their dorsal vagal state could be causing them to break connections with you, other people, themselves and the world around them. Their neocortex and therefore **social engagement system** may be offline or limited in their functioning. Which words would you choose? For example. sleepy, bored, distant, daydreaming, still, quiet, slow...
- You could then choose one word for each state and think of these words to describe the three states for that child, for instance, Settled Sam, Squirmy Sam and Sleepy Sam (The alliteration can make the exercise fun, but it isn't essential!)

Doing this for each child in the class might be excessive, but for a select few children whom you know struggle with self-regulation, it may help you recognise and track their autonomic states, and therefore guide you in how to help them. Both Squirmy Sam and Sleepy Sam need cues of safety to bring them back to the Connection end of the scale. You can provide these cues through your strong ventral vagal state. Sleepy Sam needs to do something physical to activate his shutdown body. The Connection Diet activities (in Part II) would help co-regulate him and bring him back to his ventral vagal state.

If you found you were able to easily choose words to describe the atmosphere of the class in the Tracking Autonomic States questions earlier, and you found the words were together on the Connection-Protection scale, you might find the renaming autonomic states idea useful for the class as a whole. You might have a Focussed Y8, Fidgety Y8 and Floppy Y8!

In Chapter 5 we will be looking at exercises to get to know your own autonomic states, which could be adapted to tracking the autonomic states of your classes and your pupils.

Summary

Learning Points

- The Connection-Protection continuum is a useful tool for understanding a child's challenging behaviour.
- Challenging behaviour can be viewed as a communication and an attempt to meet an unmet need.
- Maslow's Hierarchy of Needs provides a model for identifying five levels of human needs. The most basic needs in the model are worth considering when exploring the purpose of the child's challenging behaviour.
- Another way of viewing challenging behaviour is as a maladaptive strategy to manage overwhelming feelings, i.e., an ineffective attempt at self-regulation.
- The COVID-19 pandemic caused increased anxiety in adults and children and impacted aspects of the development of children and young people worldwide.
- Anxiety can present in many different ways in children and young people.
- Children and young people who are autistic and/or have other neurodevelopmental conditions, who struggle with self-regulation, can be helped using Polyvagal Theory in the same way as all children, i.e., by using the strong ventral vagal state of the adult and providing unconscious cues of safety from the adult's ANS to the child's ANS.
- Tracking autonomic states of pupils and groups of pupil can give insight into the child's experience and guide us in how to help the child. Renaming the autonomic states is one strategy for tracking them.

5 Getting to Know Your Autonomic Nervous System

In Chapter 6, we will be looking at ways to calm a dysregulated child. The most powerful tool you have for this challenge is your own **autonomic nervous system** (ANS). This chapter may feel like it's focused on self-help, and managing your own emotional wellbeing, but it is essential reading for what will follow, as you will be exploring your own **self-regulation** and strengthening your **ventral vagal state**, in preparation for managing the dysregulated child. There are exercises throughout this chapter, as well as at the end.

Self-regulation is key. A dysregulated adult cannot regulate a dysregulated child. In order to self-regulate, you need good awareness of your own **autonomic states**. If you are aware that you are in a **blended state** and you can feel **sympathetic mobilisation** or **dorsal shutdown** is starting to take control, you need strategies to keep your ventral vagal state online and strong. The aim of this chapter is to give you a firmer footing in your ventral vagal state, so you will find it easier at those times when sympathetic mobilisation or dorsal shutdown have been activated. This is like strengthening a muscle ready for the times you'll really need it, and as with muscles, regular exercise is the way to build that strength. We will explore activities that you can easily fit into your daily and weekly routines to give you more time in your ventral vagal state. Not only should this make you feel better prepared to deal with dysregulated young people, but it should also reduce your stress levels, and help you feel more grounded and more confident in your skills.

Most of the sections are focused on self-regulation, apart from The Power of Pets, which uses unconscious ANS communication with other mammals to co-regulate. The first section, however, is focused on *identifying* and *tracking* autonomic states, as this is the starting point for tuning in to your ANS.

ANS Tracking

To help you befriend your autonomic nervous system, we will explore creative ways to identify the state you are in, then different ways to track your states:

DOI: 10.4324/9781003396574-7

- One useful strategy for identifying the three autonomic states is to give them alternative representations, that make more sense of what they feel like. In Chapter 4, we looked at *renaming* the states for individual pupils. This is one idea you could use for yourself.
- Another way of thinking about the three states, might be to *visualise* or even find pictures of a place or environment to represent each state. Maybe for you the ventral vagal state feels like being on a beach on holiday, sympathetic mobilisation is like a crowded supermarket, and dorsal shutdown is a swampy marshland. Or maybe the three states feel like different weather – ventral vagal as warm sun with a gentle breeze, sympathetic mobilisation as thunder and lightning, and dorsal shutdown as cold quiet snow. Or maybe they feel like different seasons.
- You might find the autonomic states can be presented very simply as *shapes*, *colours*, or *textures*. Maybe ventral vagal is green and soft, sympathetic mobilisation is red and prickly, and dorsal shutdown is black and smooth.
- For some people, *sound* works better. You could choose particular songs or pieces of music for each state, or particular sounds. Ventral vagal might be a gentle piano piece or the sound of birds singing, sympathetic may be heavy metal music or the sound of an alarm, dorsal shutdown might be silence or a low hum.

Take some time to try one or more of these ideas, or find your own way of describing the states, that feels right for you. Once you feel more comfortable with what each state feels like, identifying and tracking your states will become easier.

Let us try now with a simple exercise in self-awareness (you might want to do this exercise on paper).

Notice what your body is feeling like right now as you read – are there different sensations in different parts of your body? Is there any tension anywhere? How *connected* do you feel to your body? Is it difficult to identify sensations? On the Connection-Protection scale, mark where you feel you are right now. Remember the Connection end is not only about connecting to others, but also about your own *mind-body* connection.

Connection ←---→ **Protection**

When you feel more connected to your body, you can *identify* your autonomic state more easily, and have more control over it. What is your current autonomic state? Ventral vagal? blended? Use your ideas for representing the autonomic states from above, to help you identify the state you are in.

There are different ways you can *track* your autonomic state. We will look at a few here, and I would suggest choosing one that feels like a good fit for you.

You could consider the three autonomic states as scales, where you circle where you are at on each scale, but the total must add up to ten:

Ventral vagal	0 - 1 - 2 - 3 - 4 - 5 - 6 - 7 - 8 - 9 - 10
Sympathetic mobilisation	0 - 1 - 2 - 3 - 4 - 5 - 6 - 7 - 8 - 9 - 10
Dorsal shutdown	0 - 1 - 2 - 3 - 4 - 5 - 6 - 7 - 8 - 9 - 10

Think of a lesson that was particularly challenging. How strong was your ventral vagal state from 0 to 10? Circle the number on the scale. If you circled 6, you might have had the remainder (4) as sympathetic mobilisation or dorsal shutdown. Here we are looking at the amount of activation of each state.

You might want to replace the names of the three states with your own ideas from above, for instance:

Holiday beach	0 - 1 - 2 - 3 - 4 - 5 - 6 - 7 - 8 - 9 - 10
Crowded supermarket	0 - 1 - 2 - 3 - 4 - 5 - 6 - 7 - 8 - 9 - 10
Swampy marshland	0 - 1 - 2 - 3 - 4 - 5 - 6 - 7 - 8 - 9 - 10

Another visual representation could be using something resembling a pie-chart. Your ANS, as a whole, is a single circle, like a dial. In that challenging lesson, how much of your ANS was in ventral vagal, and how much in another state? See Figure 5.1 for an example.

Using words instead of images and numbers can suit some people better. On the Connection-Protection scale, label different points on the scale with words that fit how that state feels. For instance, you may have words or phrases like *tuned in, open, chatty, focused* near the Connection end, words like *uncertain, edgy, tentative* may appear near the middle, and words like *walled, attacking, small, avoiding* towards the Protection end. Of course, it doesn't have to be words: maybe colours are more meaningful for you. You could make the Connection-Protection scale into a colour scale.

Choose the best way for you to represent your autonomic states and your preferred way of tracking them and have a go at identifying your states each day for a week, or maybe each lesson for a day. This is the start of training your mind to tune in to your ANS and notice your autonomic states.

Next, we will look at strategies for strengthening your ventral vagal state, so sympathetic mobilisation and/or dorsal shutdown are less able to take control.

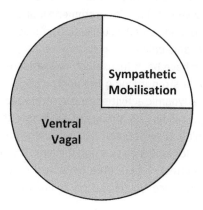

Figure 5.1 Pie chart shaded to show a blended state of ventral vagal and sympathetic mobilisation

Body and Breathing

Connecting well with the body and the breath brings us into the present moment. Often sympathetic mobilisation and dorsal shutdown at times when you are in no danger, are about bad experiences from the past or worries of what might happen in the future. If you are in a safe place and there is no threat, then your body's survival response is not needed. Bringing yourself into the present moment helps to deactivate the survival response and strengthen the ventral vagal state. One way to achieve this is by focusing on the body and your breathing.

Earlier I suggested noticing the sensations in your body and identify any tension, etc., in order to identify your autonomic state. This **body tracking** can be taken much further and can become a form of meditation or mindfulness.

Try starting at the top of your head and working down your body to your toes. Place your focus on your scalp, notice any sensations - hot, cold, tightness, movement of the air, then slowly move down to your forehead, staying for a moment to really focus on how it feels. Now moving steadily down your face, try squeezing your eyes shut then opening them to really focus your attention on the sensations. Continue in this manner, to your neck, shoulders, arms, hands, back, torso, legs and finally feet. Take it slow and really focus on each part of your body. Now try adding in some gentle movements or stretches and focus on how they feel in different parts of your body. Really concentrate on the sensations. You might like to include massage in this exercise. Try simply massaging one hand with the other, maybe using scented hand cream. Focus your attention on the sensation in your hands and the fragrance of the hand cream.

Another exercise to focus the mind on the body is to focus on breathing. This is often the first step in bringing the mind to a meditative state. There are many different breathing exercises, sometimes involving counting or visualising the breathing cycle as a shape. Try now, simply noticing breathing in and breathing out.

Exercises such as these can be easier when they are guided. Popular apps such as Headspace and Calm can be extremely helpful in providing guided exercises for focusing the mind on the body and the breath. Another guided approach could be attending a yoga class (in person or virtually), where you are encouraged to notice your breath as you move, and to tune in to how your body feels with the movements. I would recommend looking online for guided breathing exercises, guided meditations, and guided visualisations. Aside from the popular apps, there are many free resources available online.

These suggestions, so far, have been focused on relaxation exercises, but improving the connection with the body and strengthening the ventral vagal state can also be achieved through higher-energy, more dynamic activities. The ventral vagal state can be strengthened simply by breathing in deeply, and by breathing out for longer than we breathe in, and this can be accomplished by singing. Have you noticed that when you sing, you breathe in deeply and quickly, then breathe out for longer as you sing the lyrics? Singing strengthens your ventral vagal state, simply by its effect on your breathing. Next time you feel some sympathetic mobilisation activation, for instance, you're feeling anxious or agitated, put your favourite track on, and sing!

Another high-energy approach to connecting with your body and your breath, is through sports and physical exercise. If you enjoy playing football, running, working out at the gym, going to fitness classes, these are all great ways to really connect with your body and regulate your breathing, thereby strengthening your ventral vagal state. You may be aware that exercise is said to be good for mental health as well as physical health. When you exercise, your mind is on the activity, and on how your body feels. You can feel the strength of your muscles, the fullness of your lungs and the power of your heart. If you don't enjoy high-energy exercise, walking can have a similar effect, as you can still feel an increase in your heartrate and breathing rate, and you can focus on the strength in your legs with each step. The activation of the ventral vagal state through exercise can reduce anxiety and stress, as these are emotions associated with sympathetic mobilisation.

There are probably far more activities than I have described here that strengthen the mind-body connection, but there is one more I have to mention before we move on, and that's 'Power Poses'! Sometimes they are considered just a bit of fun, and to not have any real benefit to how you feel, but when considering how to strengthen the ventral vagal state, I do think they have some value. The most common power pose is the superman pose, but the warrior poses from yoga can also be quite effective, and I think the real power comes from noticing how your body feels while standing in the pose. Power poses promote the mind-body connection. Try it now – stand with your feet at shoulders width apart, hands on your hips, drop your shoulders, stand as tall as you can, head held high. Notice the strength in your arms and legs, notice how tall you are, notice how big your lungs are when you breathe in, notice how solid you are on the ground. How do you feel?

Regulation through Rhythm

I recently discovered the benefits of running, not only to my physical health, but in strengthening my own ventral vagal state. I started with the popular 'Couch to 5K' app, and now I run regularly. One thing I noticed, once I was fit enough to run comfortably, was the almost hypnotic sound of my feet hitting the ground accompanied by the rhythm of my breathing. I found myself in something of a daze listening to the rhythm – breathe in, step, step, step, breathe out, step, step, step, breathe in, step, step, step ... and I discovered a very calming effect on my mind.

We are programmed to seek out rhythm, as it has a soothing regulating effect. Our first moments of being, before we are even born, we are hearing and feeling the rhythm of our mother's heartbeat. Babies are gently rocked with a regular rhythm to calm them and send them to sleep. Rhythm can help regulate breathing and heartrate, and it can be found in so many places and in so many forms. One obvious source of rhythm is music – whether you are listening, singing, or dancing (or all three), the rhythm can have a calming influence. There are, however, many other sources of rhythmic sounds and movements, such as listening to the sounds of waves crashing on the beach, swinging or rocking, for example, in a hammock or rocking chair, walking at a steady pace, repetitive hand movements when knitting, feeling a cat purring as you stroke it. Take a moment to think of the rhythms you come across in your typical day and notice how they make you feel.

Sensory Soothing

Another discovery I made with my new hobby of running, was the sensory input. I often ran early in the morning, when the birds are singing, and the air smells fresh and feels cool on my skin. Consciously noticing what my senses were detecting brought me into the present and helped my connection with my body.

Many of the examples above have sensory aspects, such as stroking a cat, using scented hand cream, listening to music. Consider the five main senses – hearing, sight, touch, smell, and taste, and imagine these two things you do every day: eating and brushing your teeth. You use ALL your senses in these two activities, but do you really *notice* the sensory input? Next time you do one of these activities, pay close attention to your senses – what does your food look like? What are the sounds coming from your mouth? What textures can you feel against your tongue and inside your cheeks? What does it smell like? What does it taste like? Notice all your senses. This is an example of mindfulness, which is something we will explore in more detail in the next section.

Consider now *your* most comforting and calming sensory experiences, and think about all your senses. They may be the smell of your dog, the feeling of warm water, the sound of your children laughing, the taste of chocolate, looking at a favourite photo, the aroma of roast dinner cooking, the sound of water flowing in a stream, the feeling of snuggling in a soft blanket, watching the sun setting. Focusing on positive sensory experience further strengthens your mind-body connection and therefore your ventral vagal state.

Mindful Moments

The example above of noticing the sensory experience of eating or brushing your teeth was a description of how to be 'mindful'. Mindfulness is about being in the present moment and really noticing what is happening in the here and now, internally and/or externally. Mindfulness can be practised anywhere at any time, but its best done when you are not needing to concentrate on an important task, such as driving or teaching. You can practise mindfulness this very moment, although it would require you to stop reading!

As Andy Puddicombe, creator of the Headspace app, explains: 'Mindfulness means to be present, aware of what you're doing and where you are. You don't have to do anything differently from how you would normally do it. The only thing you need to do is be aware' (2011, p. 107).

Nature provides us with a rich source of sensory information and is an ideal place to try out mindfulness if it is something new to you. Next time you are outside experiencing nature, try a few moments of mindfulness. You don't need to be immersed in nature and you don't need to spend lots of time, for these few moments to have value – simply stopping for two minutes next to a tree can provide enough nature for this mindfulness practice. Pay attention to *all* your senses, just as in the example above. First look closely at your tree – the colour of the bark, the movement of the leaves. Now listen for any birds singing, a breeze through the leaves, any other sounds. Touch the bark, the branches, the leaves and notice the different textures. Taste and smell the air at this place – notice whether it is different from indoors. Focus on the here and now, and everything your senses are picking up.

If you are someone who enjoys gardening or walking your dog, you will find plentiful opportunities for moments of mindfulness, without needing to make extra time for it. It's just a case of remembering and making it a part of the activity.

Brain Workouts and Being Your Best Friend

So far, we have looked at strategies for strengthening the ventral vagal state, which involve focusing on the body which then influences the mind, but we can achieve the same result, by using the higher-thinking brain (the **neocortex**) to influence the body. Consciously activating the neocortex can quieten the **limbic system**, thereby reducing the intensity of emotions. Here we will look at two ways of using our neocortex – higher-thinking tasks that take concentration (brain workouts), and use of language to influence how you are feeling (being your best friend).

Brain workouts are very much a matter of personal preference and are not for everyone, but if you can find an activity that works for you, it can activate your neocortex and therefore strengthen your ventral vagal state. Examples of activities that require neocortex functioning include crosswords, jigsaw puzzles, word games, reading, wordsearches, sudoku and logic puzzles. There are also many apps and online games that use higher thinking, such as Tetris, CandyCrush, strategy games and brain training apps.

'Being your best friend' is about finding words that can help you self-regulate at times when you are starting to feel dysregulated. This can be achieved through positive self-talk, as though you were giving a pep-talk to someone you care for, or maybe through finding song lyrics that you connect strongly with, or finding yourself a mantra you could repeat to yourself.

Consider now a situation that makes you anxious, maybe a challenging lesson or a difficult meeting. What is your self-talk? Do you find you are saying things like 'I hate this lesson; it never goes well; I just want it to be over', 'I'll have to be really assertive in this meeting but I know I won't find the right words; they won't listen to me; we'll never reach an agreement'. This sort of self-talk is common and is fed by anxiety, but it is not likely to help you. Positive self-talk can reduce your survival responses of sympathetic mobilisation and dorsal shutdown, and strengthen your ventral vagal state, so you go into the lesson or the meeting feeling more confident, self-assured, and grounded. Positive self-talk for these scenarios might include: 'I know it might be difficult, but I'm a good teacher; I've had plenty of good lessons, I can do this' and 'my opinion is important, I'll speak clearly and confidently; even if people can't agree, we'll find a way through'. Positive self-talk can be difficult, especially if stress, anxiety, and self-doubt are taking over, but if you take a step back and think of what you would say if your best friend was asking for your reassurance, it'll be easier to find the words that will help. Take a moment to think about what your self-talk sounds like. Does it help you? Is it what you would say to someone you care about, who was asking for your help?

You may find that sometimes a song really seems to speak to you and that certain lyrics stay with you. These may be lyrics that resonate with a familiar feeling, or they may be uplifting lyrics that make you feel good. When you think of those lyrics, you might find the song starts playing in your head, then you have the added benefit of the melody and beat. Bringing to mind helpful song lyrics can activate parts of the neocortex and help with self-regulation. For example, 'You shoot me down, but I won't fall, I am titanium'; 'we are the champions, my friends, and we'll keep on fighting till the end'; 'I get knocked down, but I get up again, you are never gonna keep me down.' What are *your* self-affirming, inspiring or uplifting song lyrics?

Another use of meaningful words is in mantras, which are short phrases that can be repeated over and over. The repetition has a soothing effect similar to the effect of rhythms. Some examples of mantras include 'I am enough'; 'I love myself, I believe in myself, I support myself'; 'Everything I need is within me', or a mantra could simply be one word, such as 'breathe' or 'calm'. The best mantra for you will be the one you find or create for yourself that you really connect with.

Calming Creativity

Doing something creative, in any form, involves different areas of the brain, but predominantly the neocortex, as it requires focus. Creativity can provide an effective means of expressing and making sense of emotions, especially those challenging emotions associated with the survival response, such as anxiety, fear, anger, helplessness, panic and despair. You may already have a creative outlet that you are familiar with, and you find useful as a calming or self-regulating activity. There are many forms of creativity worth exploring and experimenting with: drawing, jewellery making, interior design, painting, creative writing, photography, song writing, embroidery, playing an instrument, collage, sculpting, cooking, acting, scrapbooking, writing poetry, dancing, knitting, gardening, sewing, making models, computer animation, upcycling clothes or furniture, etc., nail art, origami, pottery, decoupage ... and the list goes on. Whether you have a creative outlet or not, try something new to see how it feels and whether it could give you more time in your ventral vagal state.

The Power of Pets

In Chapter 1, we looked at the **triune brain**, which showed the three main parts of the human brain. The middle part is the limbic system, also known as the **mammalian brain**, as it is common to all mammals. This part of the brain is associated with emotions, social behaviour and attachment - things we have in common with most other mammals. If you have a dog or a cat, you will be familiar with interpreting their emotional state, seeing their social behaviour and feeling their attachment to you. You can tell what mood your pet is in, despite it not being able to use words to tell you. Somehow, we know a cat purring is relaxed and content, and a dog wagging its tail is happy. Because you have an attachment to your pet, you will also know all the subtle behaviours that give away your pet's feelings. That's the non-verbal communication between your pet's ANS and yours. Your ANS and your pet's ANS will be constantly talking to each other. Just as you can understand your pet, to a certain extent it can understand you too. Dogs are particularly adept at sensing the emotional states of people, especially their owners, as they have an attachment to them. They respond to their owners with care and **empathy**. They love unconditionally without judgement, they live in the present moment, and they form strong attachments to their pack, I.e., their family. With such a strong emotional connection and feeling of support, it's no wonder we refer to our pets as part of the family.

One of the particularly helpful aspects of having a pet is that they are usually experts at self-regulation, and are therefore good at **co-regulation**. How does your dog react if you are upset? Does it rest its head on your lap? Spending time with animals, especially mammals, can be an effective means of emotional regulation, as they activate the social engagement system in the neocortex, thereby strengthening ventral vagal activation. They also increase levels of oxytocin (the love hormone) and reduce cortisol (the stress hormone). I don't have any pets myself, but I always stop to say hello to the friendly cats that live along my running route, and they always put a smile on my face. You don't have to have a pet to find ways to benefit from the powerful co-regulation of animals.

Summary

Learning Points

- The first stage in tuning in to your own autonomic nervous system is to practise identifying your three states. This can be made easier by using creative ideas.
- The second stage in connecting with your ANS is tracking your autonomic states, which can be achieved by various means.
- Connecting with body and breath can strengthen your ventral vagal state. Examples include body tracking, singing, exercise and power poses.
- Rhythm can have a soothing effect on the nervous system, and can be found in many places, such as music, movements and sounds.
- Focusing on the five main senses (sight, hearing, taste, touch and smell) can strengthen the connection with the body and help with self-regulation.
- Practising mindfulness brings us into the present moment and is a powerful means of self-regulation. A good place to practise mindfulness is in nature.
- Brain workouts activate the neocortex and therefore strengthen the ventral vagal state. Examples include logic games, word puzzles and reading.
- Being your best friend is another means of using the neocortex to regulate the nervous system. Suggestions include positive self-talk, uplifting song lyrics and mantras.
- Creativity activates the neocortex, but also provides a means of expressing and processing emotions.
- Connecting with animals, especially pets, can provide co-regulation, in a similar way to connecting with other people.

Practical Exercise

There have been exercises to try throughout this chapter. Now we can put together the ideas that work for you:

- Decide on the most meaningful way you can describe and connect with your auto-nomic states, and try tracking them for a day, or at a few times in a week. This will help you tune in to your ANS.
- Thinking back to the strategies discussed for strengthening your ventral vagal state, look for ideas that can be *combined* and can easily fit into your daily and weekly routine. For instance, if you walk your dog every morning, maybe you can

practise mindfulness by focusing on your senses on your walk, notice the rhythm of your steps, and notice how it feels to connect with your dog. Maybe you could listen to music as you cook dinner, sing along, notice how your body feels as you move in time to the music, and mindfully notice the aroma of the food. Make a little plan of times in your week where you can consciously practise these strategies, and really notice the feeling of being in your ventral vagal state.

- Make a plan for the times when you feel your body moving into sympathetic mobilisation or dorsal shutdown, to help you self-regulate. For instance, stand in a power pose for a couple of minutes, massage your hands with strong scented hand cream, focus on the rhythm of your breathing and consciously breathe slower and deeper, drink cold water and notice the feeling inside your body as you swallow, say a meaningful mantra to yourself. At times when the body's survival responses are taking over, it can be very difficult to remember the things that help, because the neocortex stops working as efficiently, so it might be a good idea to jot down the strategies in preparation for these times.

6 Calming the Dysregulated Child

This chapter is focused on how to deal with the dysregulated child in the moment, using your connection to your own **autonomic nervous system** (ANS). You'll notice that this chapter is relatively short. This is intentional, so you can quickly re-read it when you need a reminder of the approach, such as before a day when you have 'that lesson' that always brings its challenges. Before you read this chapter, I strongly advise that you fully digest Chapter 5. Practise **attuning** to your ANS and strengthening your **ventral vagal state**. Developing your capacity for **self-regulation** is essential for co-regulating an emotionally overwhelmed child or young person. In this chapter, we will explore a three-stage approach to calming a dysregulated child, focused on using your own ANS:

Be Safe → Feel Safe → Connect

Be Safe: Removing the Threat

Being safe and *feeling* safe are not the same thing, which is why these two ideas are addressed separately. It is possible to be safe and still feel under threat. If there is anything the child's ANS perceives as threatening, this needs to be removed or dealt with before they can start to feel safe.

In some cases, the threat will be clear, and you will know how to deal with it, such as a physical or verbal attack from another child, a loud noise that is clearly frightening the child, or the young person being faced with a difficult academic task, such as an exam. But often the threat is not obvious.

As we explored in Chapter 3, threats can be categorised as *internal*, *external*, or *relational*. The obvious threats are usually in the external or relational categories. If the threat is not obvious to you, take a moment to consider the environment, the interactions with others around the child and what has happened leading up to the child's **dysregulation**. Removing *external* or *relational* threats may involve removing the child from the classroom or removing other children from the vicinity. It may mean taking the difficult work off the desk or turning the volume down on the video that's playing, or turning the light back off or on, or it might

DOI: 10.4324/9781003396574-8

involve taking the child outside so they can get away from the smell of lunch cooking. Once you have identified the threat, you can work on a solution to remove it.

The threats which are hardest for us to see may be *internal*. Of course, if the child is experiencing an internal sensation that is being read by their ANS as a threat, our capacity for identifying and removing the threat is extremely limited. Here's where we need to be creative and think outside the box. Knowledge of the child is invaluable at times like this. For instance, if you know that the feeling of being too hot is a sensation that sends this child into sympathetic mobilisation, you might first need to encourage the child to drink some cold water and sit in a cool place.

You may also remember from Chapter 3, that Lisa Dion suggested *unknowns* and *unrealistic expectations* as types of threat. Is the threat unexpectedly having a supply teacher taking the class? Or a change to the timetable? Or a school trip? (These are all unknowns.) Maybe the child is hearing 'shoulds' that are being perceived as threats, as they feel like expectations that they cannot meet: "You should know how to line up properly at your age"; "You shouldn't be talking when I am talking"; "You should know not to call other children mean names". If you find yourself saying 'should' statements, consider how they are heard by the child. Are these *realistic* expectations for this particular child in the emotional state they are in right now? How do these statements impact the child's self-esteem and sense of who they are?

Another less obvious type of threat is *incongruence*, which we have examined in previous chapters. Remember your ANS gives away your autonomic state by sending unconscious signals to the child's ANS, and you can't fool the child's ANS. Tune in to your ANS and activate your ventral vagal state, so your ANS sends cues of safety to the child. Be authentic, faking it won't work. The next stage in the approach, *'Feel Safe'*, explores this idea in more detail.

Feel Safe: Tuning in to Your Own ANS

In order for the child to feel safe, their ANS needs to receive unconscious cues of safety. As the adult helping this child, it is your ventral vagal state that will provide these cues of safety, so you need to be securely in your strong ventral vagal state. Chapter 5 detailed ways to connect with your ANS and strengthen your ventral vagal state. If you dive into this situation before attuning to your own autonomic state, you are likely to react rather than respond. There is an important distinction to be made here. When faced with a challenging situation, we can easily find ourselves reacting without much forethought, which means the child's unconscious cues of threat have been read by our own ANS and we have acted upon them as though we are also under threat. When we take a moment to consider the situation, attune to our own ANS and self-regulate, we can respond to the child in a measured way. We then have some control over the unconscious messages being sent to the child.

This can be a difficult skill to learn. As with any skill, some people pick it up very quickly and some need to practise more. If you are finding it difficult to stop yourself stepping straight in and *reacting*, I would recommend starting by *reflecting* on situations where you have been faced with a dysregulated child. Take yourself back to the moment before you acted and see if you can identify where your autonomic state was. It may have been **blended** ventral vagal and **sympathetic mobilisation**, especially if the child was going into fight, flight, or freeze.

Can you remember what your breathing was like? Was your heart beating faster? Visualise yourself in that same situation, taking a deep breath. Now visualise using the strategies you learnt from Chapter 5 to self-regulate, before you approach the child. Practising this skill as a thought-exercise is the first step towards making it a reality.

Consider these three questions in that moment before you respond:

- What is happening in my body? (breathing, heartrate, muscle tension, etc.)
- What am I feeling? (anxious? frightened? numb? angry?)
- What are my thoughts/self-talk? (remember your thoughts and self-talk influence how you are feeling.)

Now use whatever strategy you have identified from Chapter 5 that works best for you, to strengthen your ventral vagal state and keep you regulated.

Connect: Body Tracking, Breathing, Moving

Now you are feeling confident and in control, it is time to step in and approach the dysregulated child, and the goal here is *connection*.

We are looking at two types of connection: (1) connecting the child's mind with their body; and (2) connecting the child to another person, i.e., you. Both these connections activate the ventral vagal state.

The mind-body connection can be strengthened by **body tracking**. Notice aloud what is happening for the child's body. For instance, 'I can see that your hands are making tight fists'; 'it looks like your arms and legs have lots of energy and want to move'; 'I can see that you've made your body into a tiny ball and you're hiding your face'. This helps the child notice what their body is doing. In an overwhelmed state, they may have very little awareness of their own body.

You can also model this with your own mind-body connection. Notice aloud what your body is doing. For instance, with your hand on your heart, 'I can feel my heart is beating fast, I wonder if yours is too'; 'I've noticed that my hands are shaking a bit, I'm going to open and close my hands a few times because I know that helps'; 'I feel like my body doesn't want to move at all, so I'm going to make myself stand up and stretch out my arms'; 'I've noticed that you are holding your breath. I'm going to take a deep breath, then breathe out slowly as though I'm blowing out candles on a birthday cake'. **Mirror neurones** come into play with examples such as these. The child will have neurones that mirror yours so when you make a movement and the associated neurones in your brain fire, the corresponding neurones in the child's brain also fire and then, to some extent, *they* benefit from the actions *you* are making. With younger children, you might even notice them mimicking your movements without realising it as their mirror neurones fire.

By naming these experiences for yourself and the child, you are also activating their **social engagement system**, so you are helping them connect with you. If the child is in a blended state of ventral vagal and either sympathetic mobilisation or dorsal shutdown, then they may be able to tell you what has upset them, as their social engagement system will still be online. Of course, if this is the case, you can listen and empathise, but I would still encourage the body tracking to strengthen their ventral vagal state.

If you find the child seems to have excess energy and seems to need an outlet, I recommend redirecting their energy to an activity which is contained and not destructive, such as running outside, punching pillows, kicking a football, tearing up cardboard boxes, throwing a tennis ball at a wall. You can help the child feel that their overwhelming emotions have been validated by saying things like 'I can see you're really angry. We can't throw the books. Show me another way – let's throw the basketballs outside'; 'You don't need to tear up your work for me to understand that you're upset with your test result. Show me a different way, maybe you could paint a picture to show me the feeling.' Again, statements such as these will only be really understood if the child already has some social engagement activation. If they have no ventral vagal activation, stick with the body tracking until they start to connect with you. Once the child connects with their body and with you, their social engagement system will have activated, as will their ventral vagal state. You have then co-regulated the child and they are no longer overwhelmed by their emotional state. Continue the body tracking as this will help the child gain insight into how they came out of the dysregulated state and help develop their ability to self-regulate. After the event, reflect with the child on what they had been feeling, and how their body had reacted. Help them identify what helped them feel in control again.

Sometimes we find ourselves in situations where it feels like there is no time to stop and consider our response and we dive in, trusting our instincts and experience. If you find yourself having reacted quickly, and not self-regulated before acting, it is not too late to employ the approach described here. As soon as you realise, simply stop, and take a deep breath. Body-track yourself aloud, so the child sees you self-regulating. This is valuable modelling for the child. Even if you find your actions have inadvertently escalated the situation, you can still *stop*, *breathe* and *body-track*. Once you have yourself firmly in your ventral vagal state, go back to the three-stage approach:

Be Safe → Feel Safe → Connect

Summary

Learning Points

- Take the three-stage approach: Be Safe → Feel Safe → Connect
- Be Safe: Removing the threat – consider what type of threat the child's ANS is detecting, such as internal, external or relational, or whether it is unknowns, unrealistic expectation ('shoulds') or incongruence.
- Feel Safe: Tuning in to your own ANS – Practise *responding* rather than *reacting* by taking a moment to attune to your ANS, using these questions: What is happening in my body? What am I feeling? What are my thoughts/what is my self-talk?
- Connect: Body tracking, breathing, moving – there are two connections to help the child make: their mind-body connection and their connection to you. Track your body and their body, making movements and breathe to model how you self-regulate. Redirect the child's energy. Reflect with the child on what happened in terms of their feelings and their body reactions.

- If you have found yourself having acted without following this approach, and inadvertently escalated the situation, stop, breathe and body-track yourself. Then return to the approach above.

Practical Exercise

Make a list of everything about your school that makes you safe – this is your Being Safe list, for instance 'Good security so strangers cannot get on site' and 'The car park is well lit when it's dark'. Now make a list of what makes you Feel Safe at your school. You might have 'I always teach in the same room so I know what to expect when I first arrive in my classroom', 'My colleagues smile and say hello when they see me' and 'We're always given plenty of notice of any changes to the school day.' What might these lists look like for the pupils at your school?

7 A Whole School Approach

The previous chapters in this book have been directed towards the individual teacher or staff member, working with the pupils in their class. What follows is targeted more at the leadership staff, because the benefits of applying **Polyvagal Theory** in the school setting would be significantly greater when a *whole school* approach is taken. Here we look at the application of Polyvagal Theory to the whole school community with the idea of a *group* **ventral vagal state**. We also explore steps to becoming a **Polyvagal-informed** school, and how this approach complements established approaches and programmes such as the trauma-informed and attachment-aware approaches.

The Current Climate

As discussed at the start of this book, research has shown a noticeable deterioration in the mental health of children and young people since the pandemic, with the lockdowns and school closures identified as significant factors. However, we cannot neglect the additional impact on our children of witnessing high anxiety in the adults around them for a long period of time, watching frightening news reports, being kept away from grandparents and other family members, and in many cases losing loved ones to COVID-19. All children and young people will have been affected in some way. For some, it was simply missing their friends and their freedom, for others, it was missing a special event such as the Y11 prom or a party for their 18th birthday, or the transition into Reception or from primary to secondary, or sitting their GCSE exams, and for some it was a significant disruption to their emotional and social development. As we know, for some children, being kept at home in a tense environment meant suffering abuse with no safe place to go to, and no safe person to turn to. A survey published by NHS Digital explored the mental health of children and young people in England from 2017 to 2022, and found that rates of probable mental health disorder in 7–16-year-olds increased from 1 in 9 children in 2017, to 1 in 6 by 2020, with rates then stabilising for the following two years, but for 17–19-year-olds, rates continued rising over the whole five years, from 1 in 10, to 1 in 4 (Newlove-Delgado et al., 2022). I'm sure you will agree these are alarming statistics. It's a quick calculation to determine how many pupils in your school

DOI: 10.4324/9781003396574-9

are statistically likely to have a mental health disorder. Schools are in a good position to help children and young people, but staff often find themselves lacking the skills, resources, or confidence to manage such a high level of mental health need in their pupils.

Every year school staff undergo safeguarding training and are alerted to the warning signs of possible abuse and issues relating to the wellbeing of pupils. In 2020, the Government's statutory guidance, *Keeping Children Safe in Education* (Department of Education, 2023) made explicit reference to mental health in the safeguarding of children. It advised that school staff should observe pupils and notice changes in them that could indicate deeper issues, that school staff should be aware of how traumatic experiences in a child's past can impact on their behaviour and mental health, and that concerns about a child's mental health should be raised with the Designated Safeguarding Lead. Mental health was being given higher status as a concern in the overall wellbeing of pupils. In 2021 and 2022, this guidance was updated with detailed reference to additional forms of abuse for school staff to be aware of, and more detail on the impacts of abuse. Then, in 2023, the guidance stated that schools should seek better clarification on children who are absent or missing from education, as this could be an indicator of a safeguarding concern. From my experience working in primary, secondary, and special schools, most staff are skilled at really knowing their pupils, and spotting minor changes in them, and there is certainly no lack of motivation to help pupils who are struggling.

I think it would be fair to say that there is a high level of mental health need in our schools, and staff are doing the best they can to meet the need. Many of the teachers I have spoken to are crying out for more help, either in the form of outside agencies or training to develop their own skills. The teaching and exercises in this book can help individual teachers help their pupils, but a whole school approach can bring about improved emotional wellbeing for *all* the staff and *all* the pupils, and even extend in a ripple effect to the families of the pupils and thereby the local community.

School as a Container

In Part II, in Chapter 8 of this book, you will find a large collection of Polyvagal-informed activities that staff can work through with pupils. But these lessons alone won't be enough to make the school a Polyvagal-informed school. I would suggest that for a school to act as a strong 'container' for the emotional worlds of its pupils, the whole school *ethos* needs to be considered. A school may have carefully planned procedures and a secure environment to ensure the safety of its pupils and staff, but as we know *being safe* and *feeling safe* are not the same thing. Do the pupils in your school *feel* safe? Do pupils act in ways that tell you they are closer to the Connection end of the Connection-Protection scale? Or are they closer to the Protection end, i.e., in survival mode?

Most of your pupils are probably in their ventral vagal states much of the time, socialising, enjoying all the school has to offer, learning to manage stressors with help from staff, and progressing academically. There will be some, however, with a history of challenging childhood experiences, who default to sympathetic mobilisation and/or dorsal shutdown at the slightest sign of threat. Strong containment is needed for strong emotions, and this can be achieved through the ventral vagal states of the adults.

Safety Starts at the Top

Anything which impacts on the whole school needs to start at the top, i.e., the leadership team. Sanders and Thompson (2022, p. 177) explain, 'Polyvagal-informed teachers understand that, just as one can't meditate in a war zone, their students can't learn their school lessons while in fight-or-flight or freeze-shutdown.'

This could be re-worded: Polyvagal-informed *leaders* understand that their *teaching staff* can't teach and support their pupils while in fight-or-flight or freeze-shutdown. Pupils can develop their ventral vagal states through interactions with staff, and staff can strengthen their own ventral vagal states through interactions with each other and their leaders. If a member of the leadership team is unconsciously sending out cues of threat to staff, these signals will quickly filter through to the pupils, escalating into school-wide sympathetic mobilisation and/or dorsal shutdown. It is imperative that leadership staff have strong ventral vagal states and a high capacity for self-regulation, so they radiate cues of safety to their school community. As we have explored earlier, the foundation for this is self-awareness.

If you are in a position of managing school staff, reflect for a moment on your own self-awareness, your capacity to self-regulate, and the strength of your ventral vagal state. Do the staff you manage experience a felt sense of safety when they interact with you? Do you strengthen their ventral vagal states through your cues of safety? We can all become dysregulated from time to time, experiencing activation of sympathetic mobilisation and/or dorsal shutdown. Think back to any of your moments of dysregulation, and how they may have looked to others. Did you raise your voice, or speak over people? Or shut down staff who were feeling angry? Did you walk away or hide from a challenging situation, in the hope that someone else would deal with it? Did you try to avoid difficult phone calls or conversations? Remember these are unconscious reactions to being in survival mode, meaning you were not feeling safe at these times. Recognising, acknowledging, and understanding your dysregulation reactions are essential exercises in developing good self-awareness. With better awareness of these reactions, comes more control over them, i.e., better self-regulation. A self-regulated leader in a challenging situation co-regulates those around them, sending out cues of safety, and thereby strengthening the *group* ventral vagal state. Reflect now on how you recover from moments of dysregulation, how you recover your own sense of safety and how you recover the sense of safety with those around you. Thinking back to Chapter 5, consider how you could strengthen your own ventral vagal state further, so you increase your capacity to stay in control in those challenging situations and use your strong ventral vagal state to support the ventral vagal states of those around you.

The Ventral Vagal Net

This idea of a group having a shared ventral vagal state, could be visualised as a **ventral vagal net**. Each staff member in the net is a junction or connecting point, with lines of connection to those around them. Figure 7.1 shows a team with a strong ventral vagal net, represented by many connectors between staff, and the staff quite close together.

This net is the 'container' holding the pupils. The role of the leaders is not only to be part of the net, but to *strengthen the connections* within the net. School leaders should have an

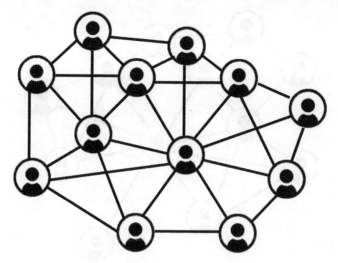

Figure 7.1 A strong ventral vagal net, showing many connections between staff members

overview of how their staff are doing, as they have responsibility for the wellbeing of both the staff and pupils in their school. This should mean they can evaluate how strong the ventral vagal net is overall and identify any individual staff member who has few connections or somewhat weak connections within the net. Figure 7.2 shows the same net as in Figure 7.1, but with far fewer connectors and with staff further apart, showing both fewer and poorer supportive relationships.

As you can see, this net would not make a strong container for the pupils. With fewer or weaker connections, the staff may find themselves more often in blended states of ventral

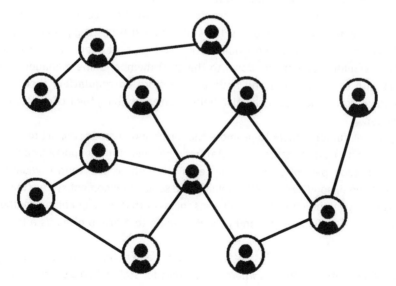

Figure 7.2 A weak ventral vagal net, showing few connections between staff members

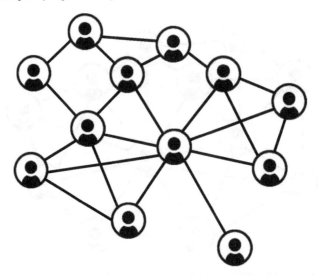

Figure 7.3 A strong ventral vagal net, with one staff member having fewer connectors

vagal with sympathetic mobilisation and/or dorsal shutdown, in other words, in defensive states, focused more on self-protection. In these states, staff are less effective at connecting with their pupils and are sending out unconscious cues of threat. Pupils themselves then have their survival states activated, and start moving towards the Protection end of the Connection-Protection scale. Team-building exercises for staff can be a great help in building supportive relationships, but I would propose that the people who know best what they need to make the net stronger are the staff members themselves. If you feel your staff ventral vagal net needs strengthening, ask the staff for their ideas.

The ventral vagal net is only as strong as the weakest connections (Figure 7.3). A strong net can be weakened in areas. If a staff member was struggling (which happens to us all from time to time), who would notice and support them? In a strong ventral vagal net, it wouldn't be entirely down to the staff member's line manager. If they are struggling with self-regulation and need a little more **co-regulation**, then colleagues with strong ventral vagal states can also help by strengthening their connections to that staff member.

It may be helpful for leaders to promote the formation of small support teams, to build stronger connections and ensure every staff member feels fully supported, safe and 'held' by the net. Feeling part of a supportive team strengthens the ventral vagal state. As Sanders and Thompson (2022, p. 211) explain, 'The social engagement system makes team-work possible by inhibiting our defensive instincts so that we can come together in the service of nurture, collaboration, and play. Belonging to a group gives us a felt sense of safety.'

Let us consider some scenarios to demonstrate the benefits of support teams within a ventral vagal net. First, a situation where the support for staff within a school was poor.

Friday. Last lesson of the day – Y10 BTEC Science. Irena dreaded it every week, but she didn't like to bother her colleagues with her worry as they all had their own stresses. Recently the boys in this class had started becoming too rowdy and she worried about something dangerous happening. Most of the girls found the boys' disruptive behaviour entertaining and egged them on, but there was a small group of quiet timid girls at the back who always looked scared of the boys. These girls creep into the class first. 'Afternoon, girls', Irena smiles faintly, they glance at her on their way to the back corner bench. She can already hear the rest of her class heading down the corridor. They bustle in noisily, knocking over chairs, sliding across the desktops, throwing their bags across the room. Irena can feel her heart pounding, as she calls out for them to settle down. They ignore her. She's been ignored so many times, she's given up on trying to get them to listen to her. She writes the task on the board and stands behind her desk wondering what she should do next, her breathing fast, her face hot. The quiet girls at the back are writing the task in their books, and have started opening their textbooks, when two of the boys head over to them. No! thinks Irena, I'm not having you frighten them any longer. She marches over to the back bench 'Sit down!' she shouts at the boys. 'Or what?' the boys turn to face her, squaring up, stepping forward. Irena recoils. She's trembling. The rest of the room has suddenly gone silent. 'The head's office, now,' she says in a shaky voice. The boys smirk, then go back to their seats, ignoring her instruction. The noise starts up again.

At this school, there is always a senior member of staff patrolling the corridors during lesson time, so Irena opens her door in the hope of catching them to seek their help. After another ten minutes of the boys climbing on the desks, shouting, play-fighting, etc., the deputy head, Mr Owen, looks in. He calls over to Irena to keep her class quiet or shut the door, as other classes are being disturbed by the noise. 'Hi, sir.' call the boys, 'Hi boys, well done on the match last week, that was an amazing goal at the end!' Mr Owen then looks over at Irena, 'I'll shut the door for you.' Irena's heart sinks. She sits at her desk, and focuses her attention on the clock on the wall.

Through the Polyvagal Lens …

Clearly, Irena had moved into sympathetic mobilisation as she feared real threat from this group of young people, in particular, the boys. The quiet girls at the back were attempting to hide themselves from the boys, also a sympathetic mobilisation reaction ('flight'). Irena tried to 'fight' by confronting them, and although she did protect the girls in that moment, she still did not have control of herself or the class, and the sense of threat remained. Mr Owen offered her no support whatsoever. It seemed that he failed to recognise the behaviour of the boys as being disruptive or threatening. Actually, his ANS probably did detect the cues of threat in the room, but his own poor self-awareness resulted in a response which only provided him with protection from the threat, i.e., to chat with the boys as though they were doing nothing wrong. Confronting the boys could have directed

> *their threatening behaviour towards him. He then chose to shut Irena's door, allowing him to escape the situation – again protection for himself. If other members of staff in this school, especially the leadership team, responded in similar ways, then this group of staff would be lacking connection, with everyone at the Protection end of the Connection-Protection scale. How would those quiet girls on the back bench ever feel safe in this school?*

Now let's consider a scenario where a small staff support team takes action.

> *It's the start of the day and Martin knows it's going to be hard work. He's struggling to focus on his lesson plan for Y5 maths, as his mind is so preoccupied with the conversation of last night where his husband announced that he was moving out. He barely slept and made his way to work in a daze. 'Hi, sir', his pupils were starting to wander in.*
>
> *In the classroom next door, sat the other Y5 teacher, Bev, who had noticed that Martin hadn't said hello this morning, and had arrived late, which wasn't like him. Bev had a quick chat with her LSA about the plan for the first lesson as her pupils started arriving.*
>
> *Ten minutes later, both lessons were underway. Both teachers kept their classroom doors open as was the norm at this school. Bev noticed Martin's class getting louder – it didn't sound like the noise of pupils on task, so she decided to have a quick look in to check Martin was OK. Bev signalled across the room to her LSA to take over. From the doorway of Martin's class, Bev noticed a task displayed on the whiteboard but very few pupils working. Martin was staring at his laptop screen, seemingly oblivious to the noise of his class. Bev quickly grabbed a slip of paper, jotted down a message and handed it to Martin, then spoke to the class firmly about bringing their attention back to their maths task. Martin read the note 'Take as long as you need away from the classroom – I'll look after your class. There's chocolate in the staffroom fridge! We can have a chat later.' Martin gave Bev a small smile of thanks and left the room. He headed for the staff toilets where he splashed cold water on his face. After taking a deep breath, Martin decided a square of chocolate could help and he might also benefit from the walk downstairs to the staffroom.*

Through the Polyvagal Lens …

In the arrangement at this Polyvagal-informed school, Martin and Bev were both in the same small support team so they were more consciously aware of how each other was doing. Bev noticed immediately that Martin wasn't himself and might need some extra support. Although Martin could have asked for that support, the distressing news from the night before had activated his dorsal shutdown state, moving him away from the Connection end of the Connection-Protection scale and reducing the activity of his social engagement system. In his daze, he may not have recognised that he needed support or known to ask for it. In their support

> **team, they had agreed that if someone notices a colleague struggling, they would write them a note that would help them leave the situation, so they could have time to self-regulate. As a support team they had shared their self-regulation strategies, so Bev knew the walk to the staffroom and chocolate treat would help ground Martin. They had also agreed as a team that they would have a 'debrief' chat after offering any extra support so they could allow time to listen to the colleague who was struggling and check that the support offered had been helpful. This debrief would also strengthen their connections as a group.**

So, what do the connections in the ventral vagal net look like? They are *supportive* relationships, but there's more to it than that. They are genuinely friendly interactions, ideally face-to-face to allow for all the unconscious ANS communications. They could be eye-contact with smiles, nods, and friendly hellos, as much as they could be supportive conversations. They are interactions that exude *cues of safety* between staff members. Each one of these interactions, no matter how small, strengthens the ventral vagal net holding the pupils. Do you walk into school and receive smiles and welcomes from colleagues on the way to your classroom? Do people say hello to you by name? How does it feel? If that has never happened, imagine it now and notice how it feels. It's like a gift we are sharing with each other, and it's a gift we can be giving to the pupils too. When pupils witness staff smiling at one another, they pick up on the cues of safety themselves, and of course those cues are amplified when the staff then smile at them too. Pupils are then more likely to smile at one another, sending out more cues of safety. It's the difference between pupils *being safe* and pupils *feeling safe*. This probably sounds a little too simple and idealistic for it to be effective, but this is just one small part of the bigger picture. Each one of these interactions makes the ventral vagal net stronger, and better able to hold those pupils who are constantly on the lookout for threat, and expecting danger.

Putting together these ideas in a whole school approach, your school could become Polyvagal-informed. Sanders and Thompson suggest the following steps in building a Polyvagal-informed school:

1. *Educate staff in Polyvagal Theory* – Chapter 1 in this book provides all the knowledge and understanding needed to educate a staff team, however, INSET with exercises and more detailed explanations could be beneficial. Reflecting on responses to challenging incidents and the behaviours of particular pupils can greatly aid in the understanding and application of the theory.
2. *Support the pupils' movement towards their ventral vagal state* – Part II, Chapter 8 of this book provides a large selection of activities for this purpose.
3. *Support the staff's movement towards their ventral vagal state* – Each staff member could audit their own ventral vagal-strengthening activities, then follow the advice and exercises in Chapter 5 on getting to know their own ANS and further strengthening their ventral vagal state.
4. *Scaffold the organisation's safety with ventral vagal teams* – As discussed above, these small support teams could be introduced to develop and strengthen the school's ventral vagal net.

5. *Develop a Polyvagal-informed culture and approach to leadership* – The culture becomes Polyvagal-informed as both staff and pupils are educated in how their ANS work, actively develop their capacity for self-regulation and work consistently as a community towards stronger ventral vagal states. Leaders oversee the strength of the ventral vagal net and the support teams within it. They also protect the net by detecting and responding to any external threats, for instance, making plans during the pandemic school closures.

As mentioned previously, an evaluation of the school ethos would be a good starting point to establish how much work is needed in becoming a Polyvagal-informed school. The exercise at the end of this chapter will also serve as useful tool in assessing the strength of your staff ventral vagal net.

Transitions

When a child moves from primary school to secondary school, they undergo a significant transition which can make or break their sense of safety in their new school. I have encountered many young people who have become 'anxious school refusers' due to this transition being too overwhelming.

Primary and secondary schools work together to provide transition plans, such as visits and tours, induction days during the summer term, an induction week at the start of September, and special meetings with the SENCo and other important staff members for children with any additional needs. Attention is given to building positive relationships between the new pupils and their new form tutor, finding their way around an unfamiliar big school and making sense of a complicated new timetable. From my experience with primary and secondary schools, the transition plans are generally well thought out. In terms of the analogy of the ventral vagal net, the plans arrange for a 'meeting' of the primary school net with the secondary school net. This can be a timetabling challenge as, of course, each secondary school has a number of feeder schools, and each Y6 class will have pupils transitioning to different secondary schools. Ideally the meeting of the ventral vagal nets of the child's primary school and secondary school provides fairly consistent containment for them. However, most children find this time of upheaval anxiety-provoking, as their sense of safety is under threat. As we have discussed previously, the unknown can be a significant sign of threat to the ANS, causing activation of sympathetic mobilisation and/or dorsal shutdown. Transition plans help some of the unknowns to become known, such as the layout of the school, the new form tutor, etc., but there are plenty of unknowns left to keep that sense of threat going. Most, if not all, Y6 children are anxious to some degree, as they finish Y6 and start Y7. Most are in blended states and therefore have some sense of their ventral vagal state. For some, the balance will have tipped and they'll have limited ventral vagal activation. These children will mostly be operating in survival mode, focused on self-protection. With all these heightened emotions, strong containment is paramount. My suggestion is that instead of a *meeting* of the ventral vagal nets, there needs to be an *overlap* of the nets. This would provide *extra* containment for the pupils, and hopefully catch the children becoming overwhelmed by their anxiety.

From the Polyvagal Theory perspective, consideration needs to be given to how *safe* the Y6 child *feels* during the transition period. Their new Y7 form tutor doesn't know them well and may not pick up on the signs that they are moving into sympathetic mobilisation and/or dorsal shutdown. The new teacher might simply think this is a quiet child, or an excitable child. Would it help for the Y6 teacher to be there on some of those induction days in the summer term to notice changes in their pupils and support them alongside the new Y7 form tutor? Would it help for the Y7 form tutor to spend some time in the Y6 classroom to observe their new pupils *before* the transition? Bringing key staff members from one school to the other is one way for the ventral vagal nets to overlap.

I wonder, also, how the Y6 child copes with saying goodbye to their primary school teachers they have formed attachments to, who have cared for them for seven years, and with saying goodbye to friends who are going to different secondary schools, while trying to take in all the new information about their new school. The role of the Y6 teacher at this time is more than supporting pupils in the move to a new school, they are also containing their pupil's feelings about the end of their primary school attachments. Any children who have early experiences of insecure attachments are likely to find this ending very challenging, and could easily move into sympathetic mobilisation and/or dorsal shutdown with strong feelings of loss, abandonment or rejection. The 'ending work' for these children needs to be started very soon after they have move into Y6, to give them time to work through their feelings, with robust containment from staff. Alongside talking, I would recommend creative and play activities to be used in 'ending work', to help children express their inner emotional worlds symbolically.

I have focused here on the Y6 to Y7 transition, as I have found from my experience of working with young people that it has the potential to cause the most disruption to their sense of safety. However, children and young people go through a transition every September when they move into a new year group, with new teachers and new classrooms. For some children, extra support needs to be put in place at the end of every summer term, to help them feel safe in the move up to the next class. There are also the transitions from nursery to Reception, Y11 to sixth form or college, moving from one school to another due to a house-move, 'managed move', etc. Any transition can be a challenge for the child or young person and their emotional response needs to be carefully monitored so appropriate support can be identified and provided. The overlapping ventral vagal nets model can be applied to any of these transitions. The key is the child or young person *feeling safe*.

Trauma-Informed, Attachment-Aware and Other Approaches

Implementing the ideas discussed in this book would not in any way conflict with any emotional wellbeing approach or programme you already have in your school. On the contrary, applying your understanding of Polyvagal Theory would enhance them. If your school is 'trauma-informed' or 'attachment-aware', then the staff will already have a good understanding of how to interpret a child's behaviour in the context of their past experiences. Relationships with key members of staff are prioritised, focusing on communication and a sense of security and safety. These approaches encourage activation of the pupil's **social engagement system**, and therefore activation of their ventral vagal state, and a movement towards connection. Knowledge of Polyvagal Theory and the role of the ANS gives a better understanding of why the trauma-informed and attachment-aware approaches are effective, and employing the activities from Chapter 8 in Part II of this book should complement these approaches well.

Developing the ability of staff to identify early signs of mental health difficulties is also included in these two approaches, but has more of an emphasis in 'Mental Health First Aid' training, alongside signposting to appropriate support and the development of active listening skills. For a Mental Health First Aider to be a good listener, they would need to be sending out unconscious cues of safety to the young person they are working with, which can only be possible with a strong ventral vagal state. Just as any First Aider is trained to check their own safety before helping casualties in an accident, the *Mental Health* First Aider needs to check the strength of their own ventral vagal state before helping a young person who is in a sympathetic mobilisation and/or dorsal shutdown state. A good understanding of Polyvagal Theory and its applications for the Mental Health First Aider could be extremely valuable.

Many primary schools have adopted emotional wellbeing approaches such as **Thrive** or **Zones of Regulation**, have trained staff as **ELSAs (Emotional Literacy Support Assistants)**, or have started following programmes such as My Happy Mind. Both the Thrive approach and the ELSA work involve time-limited, targeted support and encourage children to connect with their emotions. They provide a safe space for the child, and support development of self-regulation through strengthening the child's connection with themselves and with the adult working with them. These two approaches and other emotional literacy programmes tend to involve age-appropriate **psychoeducation**, develop self-awareness and encourage self-care. Improved self-awareness and self-care result in strengthening of the ventral vagal state. Zones of Regulation focus on self-awareness, where children are helped to identify which 'zone' they are in by tuning in to their own body signals and emotions. The four zones fit well with the autonomic states, where the Green zone (labelled as 'happy, focused, calm, proud') would be the ventral vagal state, Blue ('sad, bored, tired, sick') would be dorsal shutdown or blended ventral vagal/dorsal shutdown, Yellow ('worried, frustrated, silly, excited') blended ventral vagal/sympathetic mobilisation, and Red ('overjoyed, panicked, angry, terrified') almost solely sympathetic mobilisation. If a child is in the Blue, Yellow or Red zone, they are encouraged to use coping strategies to help them return to their Green zone. This approach encourages the child to connect with their body and also teaches them that having different emotions is normal. It empowers them to manage their own emotional state and thereby encourages self-regulation. Children are being taught how to bring themselves back to their ventral vagal state. Once again, knowledge of Polyvagal Theory helps our understanding of why these approaches and programmes work, and using the activities in Part II should only enhance the good work already being done.

Two activities that many primary schools use, which I think can sometimes be undervalued, are **Forest School** and the **Daily Mile**. Through the lens of Polyvagal Theory, we can see how these activities can go a long way towards helping children activate their ventral vagal states and develop their capacity for self-regulation. We know that physical activity helps us connect with our body. These are group activities so they encourage connection with others, i.e., activation of the social engagement system, especially in Forest School where children engage in group play and projects, such as den-building. Outside learning, especially involving nature and movement, can provide similar benefits to the children. Being outside helps children connect with the natural world, helping them feel grounded. It's a shame more secondary schools do not make use of these valuable activities.

Finally, I think it is worth mentioning the value of school pets. I've noticed a number of primary schools now have therapy dogs as part of their emotional wellbeing toolkit. Animals, especially mammals, can be extremely good co-regulators. Regular time spent with the school pet can help develop a child's capacity for self-regulation. Some schools have a small farm on site where the animals are tended by the pupils, or include regular visits to stables for the pupils with high social, emotional and behavioural need. Finding a space for connection with nature and animals can be tremendously beneficial to pupils and staff alike, in bringing them closer to the connection end of the Connection-Protection continuum.

I would encourage school leaders to audit the ventral vagal strengthening activities they have on offer for *all* their pupils.

Summary

Learning Points

- Recent research has shown that the mental health needs of children and young people have increased significantly in the last few years, with the impact of the COVID-19 pandemic identified as a key cause.
- A Polyvagal-informed school acts as a strong 'container' for the emotional worlds of its pupils.
- School leaders need strong ventral vagal states and a well-developed capacity for self-regulation to be good co-regulators for their staff and pupils.
- A staff *group* ventral vagal state can be visualised as a ventral vagal net, where staff members are the junctions, connecting to each other through supportive relationships. At challenging times, staff can feel co-regulated within the net through small support teams.
- There are five stages suggested for a school to become Polyvagal-informed: (1) Educate staff in Polyvagal Theory; (2) Support the pupils' movement towards their ventral vagal state; (3) Support the staff's movement towards their ventral vagal state; (4) Scaffold the organisation's safety with ventral vagal teams; and (5) Develop a Polyvagal-informed culture and approach to leadership.
- Transitions can be very challenging for pupils, especially the move from primary school to secondary school. An overlapping of the ventral vagal nets of the two schools can help children *feel* safe as they transition.
- Applying Polyvagal Theory enhances the work already being done in schools where the trauma-informed or attachment-aware approaches are in place.
- An understanding of Polyvagal Theory can help the effectiveness of Mental Health First Aiders working with children and young people.
- Knowledge of Polyvagal Theory can help Thrive practitioners, ELSAs, and staff using Zones of Regulation better understand how and why their work is of value to children, and can further enhance their skills.

- Forest School, the Daily Mile and outdoor learning are all ventral vagal strengthening activities for pupils. Applying Polyvagal Theory can improve outcomes for these activities.
- Animals, especially mammals, can be very good co-regulators and therefore help build the capacity for self-regulation in pupils.

Practical Exercise

Two exercises are included here: one for leadership staff or staff who manage a team (Heads of Year, Subject Leads, Key Stage leads, etc.), and one for staff who do not have a management role:

- This exercise is for staff who are in a management role. This needn't be only the leadership teams. You can do this exercise as a Head of Year or Subject Lead. Make a list of the staff you manage. If you manage a large team, I would suggest trying this with a small number of people, maybe just ten. Have a go at drawing a ventral vagal net. You might find this easiest on a screen so you can easily move people around. Move people closer to one another with short connectors if you feel they have a closer relationship. Remember the connectors denote supportive relationships. The purpose of this exercise is two-fold. It will highlight how well you know the staff you are managing, and it will give you a visual representation of their ventral vagal net. How strong does it look? Are there weak areas? Where might small support teams help to strengthen the net?
- This is an exercise aimed at staff members who do not manage a team, but it could be used by any member of staff. Consider the idea of the ventral vagal net, and start to construct a simple one with yourself in the centre. Surround yourself with colleagues whom you feel offer you support at those more challenging times – draw short strong connectors to the colleagues who offer the most support, and draw in those people who are supportive 'from a distance' further away from you. How does your part of your school's ventral vagal net look? Do you have enough support? *How* do your colleagues support you? How do you support your colleagues? Are there relationships you would like to nurture to increase the support, i.e., to strengthen the group ventral vagal net?

PART II

Using Polyvagal Theory with Pupils

8 Activities

Although it is helpful to the child or young person, that you can guide them to their ventral vagal state, and feel safe and calm, as described in Chapter 6, it is far more beneficial in the long run to help them develop the skills to do it for themselves. Here you will find activities for use with whole classes and small groups of ages 4–18 years, and a selection of activities for 1:1 use (the **Connection Diet**).

The activities for groups are organised into sections to help you plan a route through them. My suggestion would be a lesson a week, maybe as part of the PSHCE programme. However, I acknowledge that the timetable often has little room for flexibility and the school curriculum dictates every lesson, so it may be that the only option is to weave the activities into existing lessons. To help with this, I have included cross-curricular links for many of the main activities, and matched each activity to Bloom's Taxonomy to help identify possible learning objectives.

The activities are designed to help pupils learn about their autonomic states, develop their capacity for self-regulation, build stronger connections both with their peers and with themselves, and build stronger ventral vagal states. I recommend following the sections in order, so pupils have boundary setting established before moving into any other work, and psychoeducation needs to come next, to set the scene for the rest of the activities. You may find looping between Section 5, 'Connecting to the Body', Section 6, 'Connecting to Others' and Section 7, 'Self-Soothing' works well, as many of these activities overlap the sections.

When planning for these lessons, first identify any pupils you feel will struggle to cope with the sensitive nature of the activity in such a large group. Organise for them to spend the time somewhere else, with another member of staff doing the group activities as a much smaller group. This smaller group may need to follow a slightly different plan according to the needs and difficulties of the individuals, for instance, more time may be needed for the initial boundary-setting activities to help the pupils feel emotionally safe in the group.

Many of the activities involve art or written exercises, so I would recommend the pupils have an exercise book to work in, for instance, an A4 book of plain paper. The book could be given the title 'Understanding My Mind and Body', or maybe 'Understanding My Feelings'.

Towards the end of an activity and when changing tasks within a lesson, I strongly recommend time warnings, as you may find the pupils becoming quite emotionally involved in the activities. Pupils may need time to ground themselves before moving on or leaving to go to their next lesson. Suddenly being told to stop or hearing the bell ringing for the end of the

DOI: 10.4324/9781003396574-11

lesson, without warning, can activate sympathetic mobilisation. Let them know when they have 5 minutes left and 1 minute left. If these time warnings become a predictable part of the lesson, pupils will feel safer immersing themselves in the activities.

Although the activities give an age range and time, these are rough guides. You know your pupils best. You might find your class can handle activities designed for older children or need simpler activities. Bear in mind their developmental age, and also how the time away from their peers in the pandemic lockdowns may have impacted their social development. If you teach young people with any form of special educational needs or additional needs, you may find you need to adapt the activities. Again, you know your pupils best, trust your professional judgement and your own understanding of what you are guiding them through.

A few of the activities involve pupils using the internet, or accessing apps on smartphones/tablets, or watching a YouTube clip. You may find that these particular activities are difficult due to restrictions in your school, but I would recommend reviewing the activity to see if you can make adaptations during your lesson preparation, for instance, you may be able to find printable versions of the information.

Section 8, the 'Connection Diet' 1:1 activities are not an alternative to the group activities. These are for individual children who have a poor connection with their own body and struggle to connect with others. They are the children who spend very little time in their ventral vagal state and need 1:1 guidance in finding their way along the Connection-Protection scale from the Protection end back towards the Connection end. These activities are a separate programme, which is explained in more detail in the Connection Diet section.

A number of the activities have been adapted from other sources: 'Quality Circle Time in the Primary Classroom' (Mosley, 1996); 'Overcoming Trauma through Yoga' (Emerson and Hopper, 2011); 'Teaching Meditation to Children' (Fontana and Slack, 1997); 'Parenting with Theraplay' (Norris and Rodwell, 2017); 'Improving Sensory Processing in Traumatised Children' (Lloyd, 2016); 'Polyvagal Exercises for Safety and Connection' (Dana, 2020). I would highly recommend studying these sources should you need further ideas for activities or would like to enhance your skills in improving the emotional wellbeing of your pupils.

The activities are arranged in the following sections.

Group activities (whole class or small groups):

1. Warm-ups
2. Creating a Safe Space: Boundary Setting
3. Psychoeducation
4. Self-awareness
5. Connecting to the Body
6. Connecting to Others
7. Self-soothing

1:1 activities:

8. The Connection Diet

Section 1: Warm-Ups

At the start of a lesson based on the activities that follow, it can be useful to have a short warm-up activity, as a way of settling into the atmosphere of togetherness, sharing and emotional safety needed for the main activities. Below are some suggestions for warm-up activities, with a shared objective and context. They can be adapted for different age groups.

> **Objective**: To bring the group/class together, to focus attention, to transition into the safe space ready for the main activity.
> **Context**: Preparing the class for the lesson. Activating social engagement, thereby strengthening the ventral vagal state of all involved.
> **Age range**: 4-18 years.
> **Time**: 5-10 minutes.

If possible, sit the class in a circle for all these activities. Many of the activities from the other sections can also be done with the class sitting in a circle.

- **Clapping Game - Finding a Rhythm**: Each pupil makes one clap in turn going around the circle, until a rhythm is established - start clockwise then switch to anticlockwise. Try with each pupil making two quick claps instead of one, or alternate and see if a more complex rhythm can be found.
- **Clapping Game - Instructions**: Explain that one clap means stand up, two claps mean walk around the outside of the circle, three claps mean change direction, four claps mean stop (or make up your own instructions). You clap while the pupils follow the instructions, then you could have a child chosen to be the clapper
- **What's the Whisper**: Whisper a sentence or phrase to the person next to you, they whisper it to the next person and so on until it comes back to the start. See how the sentence/phrase has changed.
- **I Went to Market**: Complete the sentence 'I went to market and bought ...', then the next person completes the sentence with the item you chose and adds on their own item. Each person completes the sentence with all the items said so far, in the correct order. To give the game a modern twist, it could be 'I logged onto Amazon and bought ...'!
- **Sausages!**: Explain to the class that the rule for this game is that the answer to every questions has to be 'Sausages!', then ask them a question such as 'What did you brush your hair with this morning?' so they can all respond with 'Sausages!' Think of some absurd questions to get them laughing. This could be done in pairs or small groups, where the challenge is to keep a straight face.
- **Find the Pair**: For this you will need to have created pairs of picture cards, enough for each pupil to have one picture (e.g., butterfly and caterpillar, bucket and spade, a TV and remote control, fish and chips, hat and scarf). Put the cards in a container, then each pupil takes one card. Once everyone has their card, the task is to find their pair, but without speaking. This is a good starter if you plan on doing pair work in the next activity and want to mix up the class.

- **Class Rhythm**: Start by explaining that this is a noisy activity, so your signal for everyone to stop will be when you raise your hand. Ask each pupil in turn to make a rhythmic sound using their hands - it could be clapping, clicking fingers, tapping their leg/chair, etc. Now ask them all to make their sound at the same time (including you), after a while, everyone should start synchronising and forming a rhythm. If it's taking a while, you can initiate it by finding a rhythm with the pupils nearest you. Stop the class by raising your hand. This time, start with one person creating a rhythm, then the next joining in and so on, until the whole circle is taking part. This can be repeated with different people starting the rhythm.

- **Name Games**: Each pupil in turn gives themselves a name using alliteration with their first name. This could be as an animal, which they then act out or make the sound of, for instance, 'Saffron the Snake' or 'Freddie the Frog'. Alternatively, it could be an action word that they act out, such as 'Jumping Jamie', 'Asleep Alfie' or 'Crawling Carla'.

- **Group Stretches and Movements**: Take the lead, showing the pupils a stretch or movement for them to copy. This could be done sitting or standing. For instance, stretching arms upwards, lunges, crouching small then jumping up, squats, twisting at the waist, opening and closing the hands, rotating the feet, touching the toes, etc.

- **Favourite Colours**: Each pupil in turn states their favourite colour and what it is they like about that colour. Does it remind them of something? Is it the colour of something they like? Then point out something in the room of that colour for everyone to see.

Section 2: Creating a Safe Space: Boundary Setting

The activities in this chapter invite pupils to explore their emotions and their body reactions to their emotional states. This can feel quite exposing for the young people. For this reason, it is important that pupils feel emotionally safe enough to participate. It is important that, as the adult 'holding' this safe space, you feel confident in what you are doing and open to welcoming the emotional worlds of your pupils.

These are the key concepts required for the activities to feel safe:

- a non-judgemental culture
- acceptance and respect for each pupil's experience and feelings
- opportunity for pupils to be heard
- permission for pupils to ask questions
- empathy for pupils' feelings
- boundaries agreed by everyone, that are clear and fair.

The activities in this section are designed to address these concepts and establish the safe space, through agreeing rules and boundaries, ready for the more sensitive activities in the sections that follow (Table 8.1). I strongly advise that you don't skip this section, unless you have already completed similar activities with your class and feel that the emotional safety of your classroom has been firmly established.

Once you feel you have created your safe space, it is important to revisit the rules and boundaries that everyone has agreed to, especially when you are about to embark on a particularly exposing activity. Frequent reminders of what makes your pupils feel emotionally safe, will reinforce their connectedness as a group and result in better outcomes from the activities.

When your pupils feel safe as a group, their behaviour will improve, as will their academic performance, as they will experience stronger ventral vagal states, due to greater social engagement and frequent sharing of unconscious safety cues with one another. You should

Table 8.1 'Creating a Safe Space' activities mapped against Bloom's Taxonomy, with age range and cross-curricular links

Creating a Safe Space activities	*Age range*	*Bloom's Taxonomy*					
		Remember	*Understand*	*Apply*	*Analyse*	*Evaluate*	*Create*
Group Rules	4–18 years	✓	✓				
Listening and Taking Turns in Games	6–13 years				✓	✓	
Being Heard – Listening Skills	8–18 years				✓	✓	
Being Heard – The Talking Object	4–8 years		✓	✓			
Acceptance and No Judgement (KS2–4 English)	8–18 years		✓	✓	✓		✓

also notice greater acceptance, empathy and support for pupils who struggle the most with emotional regulation.

Group Rules

Objective: To establish agreed group rules for emotional safety.

Context: Establishing the ethos for respecting the needs and feelings of others in the group, by considering pupils' own social behaviours. Considering and planning for the emotional safety within the group. Activating social engagement, thereby strengthening the ventral vagal state of all involved.

Age range: 4–18 years.

Time: 20 minutes, up to an hour.

Resources: Whiteboard or equivalent, art materials.

Activity

1. Explain that in future lessons there are going to be activities about feelings (use age-appropriate language in your explanation) and we need everyone to feel safe enough to talk about their feelings. Emphasise that no-one will be made to talk if they don't want to.

2. For younger children: ask what rules we already have in school to help children feel happy and safe, e.g., no name-calling, no bullying, etc. Ask for their ideas about rules for this lesson, so children feel happy and safe. Give suggestions to help guide the discussion. Once you have established a short list of rules, hand out paper and art materials for the children to draw/paint pictures showing the rules. Make a display of their pictures along with written labels of the rules.

3. For older children and teenagers: split them into groups of 3–4, and ask them to write down on poster paper rules they think the class should have to help people feel comfortable talking about their feelings. Give them about 5–10 minutes. Ask the groups to feedback to the class their list of rules. Compile an agreed list on the whiteboard. Next, ask pupils to make the first page in their book the Group Rules page and write down the rules. They could decorate this page with drawings or designs.

You may be faced with the question of what happens if someone breaks the Group Rules. Explain that you would want to talk to them on their own to find out why they couldn't follow the rule, then, if possible, have a class discussion about whether anything needs to change in the Group Rules. If your response to rule-breaking is punitive, you are likely to activate sympathetic mobilisation in some pupils which will impact on the atmosphere of emotional safety. The key is a balance between firm boundaries and emotional support.

Listening and Taking Turns in Games

Objective: To reflect on why listening to others and taking turns help everyone feel good, even though it may be difficult.

Context: Establishing the ethos for respecting the needs and feelings of others in the group, by considering pupils' own social behaviours. Building a sense of emotional safety within the group. Activating social engagement, thereby strengthening the ventral vagal state of all involved.

Age range: 6–13 years.

Time: 30 minutes, up to an hour.

Resources: Board games or card games appropriate to the age of the pupils, that the pupils are likely to be familiar with.

Activity

1. Explain the objective of the activity. You may need to remind pupils that listening means paying attention and not interrupting, and usually means looking at the person who is speaking.
2. Split the class into groups of 4–5 and give each group a game.
3. Give them as much time as you feel they need to play their game. You could extend this part of the activity by having groups swap their games when they have finished.
4. Ask the pupils in their groups to come up with five words to describe how it feels to know others are letting you take your turn, and when people are listening to you without interrupting.
5. Feedback to the whole class – highlight words common to different groups.
6. Now ask pupils in their groups to find five words to describe how it feels to have to wait a long time for your turn and to listen to someone else when you want to speak. Point out that these may be good feelings or may be difficult feelings.
7. Again, feedback to the whole class. Acknowledge that sometimes we have difficult feelings and that's OK.
8. Ask pupils to complete these sentences, either verbally or written, then feedback to the class. You may want to give them suggestions of feelings words to use:

   When we listen to each other in my class, I feel …
   When we all take turns, I feel …

Being Heard – Listening Skills

Objective: To reflect on the experience of listening to others and of being listened to.

Context: Establishing the ethos for respecting the needs and feelings of others in the group, by considering pupils' own social behaviours. Building a sense of emotional safety within the group. Activating social engagement, thereby strengthening the ventral vagal state of all involved.

Age range: 8–18 years.

Time: Up to an hour.

Resources: Whiteboard or equivalent.

Activity

1. Recap the agreed Group Rules and explain the objective as exploring the rule about being heard in more depth.
2. Ask a volunteer to tell you about something they did yesterday (nothing too emotional) and role-play what not listening looks like, e.g., look away, start fidgeting, whisper to someone else, interrupt with something irrelevant, etc. Have fun with it!
3. Now ask the volunteer what that felt like for them and ask the class what you could have been doing instead to show you were listening.
4. Make a list on the board of suggestions for what a good listener does, such as, looking at the person speaking, paying attention to what they're saying, not interrupting.
5. Split the group into pairs – one to be the speaker and one to be the listener and try out good listening. Depending on the age of the pupils, you may want to choose a topic for them to talk about, e.g., hobbies, how they're feeling about their exams, etc. Then speaker and listener swap.
6. Feedback to the class how it feels to be listened to.
7. Ask pupils to complete this sentence, either verbally or written, then feedback to the class. You may want to give them suggestions of feelings words to use:

When I am listened to by another person, I feel ...

Being Heard – The Talking Object

Objective: To practise taking turns speaking and practise listening to others.

Context: Establishing the ethos for respecting the needs and feelings of others in the group, by considering pupils' own social behaviours. Building a sense of emotional safety within the group. Activating social engagement, thereby strengthening the ventral vagal state of all involved.

Age range: 4-8 years.

Time: 10-30 minutes.

Resources: A Talking Object, such as a teddy bear, something unusual (like the conch in *Lord of the Flies*), something sensory like a fluffy ball, a decorated talking stick, etc.

Activity

1. Introduce the Talking Object – give it a name ('Talking Ted', 'The Talking Stick', etc.). Explain that to help people listen in the circle there is a rule that only the person holding the Talking Object is allowed to talk – everyone else listens. Point out that right now you are holding the Talking Object so only you can talk.
2. Explain that you are going to pass the Talking Object around the circle, and when a pupil is holding the object, they can speak. They might want to say something about the object (what it feels like or looks like), or something they like about it, or they might not want to speak at all, and that's OK. If you need to intervene when a child is speaking, make sure you don't break the Talking Object rule, go to the child holding the object, so you can touch the object, then apologise for interrupting them. Remember, you are part of the circle, following the Talking Object rules, but you are also in charge. If you accidentally speak when not holding the Talking Object, point out that you made a mistake and correct it. Using the Talking Object can be more challenging for the teacher than the children at times!
3. Once the Talking Object has come back to you, give the class a topic to talk about, e.g., favourite food, something they're looking forward to, something good that happened

last week, favourite animal, etc. Pass the Talking Object around so everyone has a chance to talk while holding it. Once the object is back to you, praise children by name for using the Talking Object and comment on what different children have said, so they all know you have been listening to them.

4. For the third practice of using the Talking Object, explain that you are going to ask a question and pupils should put up their hand if they want to answer, then you'll give them the Talking Object. For instance, 'Who can tell me a time when you felt really excited?'. Praise children when they put their hand up, but make sure you're still holding the Talking Object when you do so!

5. Finally, ask for their feedback about what it is like using the Talking Object. Make sure you pass the Talking Object to anyone who puts their hand up. Offer something of your own experience here – if you found it challenging, own and name the feelings. This will model for the children that its OK to have difficult feelings, to own those feelings and to name them.

Acceptance and No Judgement

Objective: To experience seeing from someone else's perspective, in a non-judgemental way.
Context: Establishing the ethos for respecting the needs and feelings of others in the group, by considering pupils' own social behaviours. Building a sense of emotional safety within the group. Activating social engagement, thereby strengthening the ventral vagal state of all involved.
Cross-curricular Links: KS2-4 English (Spoken English).
Age range: 8-18 years.
Time: 20 minutes.
Resources: None.
Activity

1. Split the class into pairs – they could be friendship pairs or random pairs. They need to identify who is Person 1 and who is Person 2.
2. Explain that through chatting, Person 1 is going to find something Person 2 really likes but that Person 1 doesn't like (such as an online game, a film, a hobby or sport). Person 1 is then going to find out from Person 2 why they like this thing.
3. Person 1 will then speak to the whole class or a small group as though they like this thing and give the reasons they like it. They are speaking in the first person with statements such as 'I like this film because ...'. Emphasise that Person 1 needs to be convincing – they should not give any indications that they actually don't like this thing.
4. Back into pairs, the pupils swap roles and repeat the activity.
5. As a class, ask pupils to feedback on their experience of the activity.

    What did it feel like to talk positively about something they don't like?
    What did it feel *like listening to someone else talking non-judgmentally about the thing you like?*

Reflect on the pupils' feelings and discuss how different people in the class have different viewpoints, feelings and experiences. For emotional safety in the class, there needs to be acceptance of differences and no judgement on other people's feelings or experiences. You may need to reiterate that expressing discriminatory opinions, such as racist or homophobic views, are *not* accepted because they are harmful to others and therefore make the atmosphere emotionally *unsafe*.

Section 3: Psychoeducation

Psychoeducation, in this case, refers to the understanding of the Polyvagal Theory in simple terms. You'll notice that the activities are designed more for older children and teenagers, for the simple reason that much of the learning here requires a higher level of cognitive development (Table 8.2). The activities for younger children are brief and simple.

Animal Acting

Objective: To use imaginative play to compare the body experience of the three autonomic states.

Context: Develop understanding of the three autonomic states, using the child's natural form of communication and processing: play.

Cross-curricular Links: KS1-2 PE.

Age range: 4-8 years.

Time: 20-40 minutes.

Resources: None, but pictures of different animals may help.

Activity

1. Start by playing a simple game of the pupils guessing what animal you are pretending to be (easy ones might be a dog, a monkey or a lion).
2. Ask for volunteers to be animals for the class to guess.
3. Now talk about how sometimes when we have strong feelings, we can feel a bit like different animals, and ask the children to give examples of what animal they feel like, when they are angry/scared/relaxed. If they struggle, offer your own experience, e.g., 'I'm like a crocodile when I'm annoyed, and I snap at people', then pretend to be an annoyed crocodile.
4. Once the children have come up with some ideas, ask them to choose one animal for themselves for feeling happy and draw a picture of it.

Table 8.2 'Psychoeducation' activities mapped against Bloom's Taxonomy, with age range and cross-curricular links

Psychoeducation activities	Age range	Bloom's Taxonomy					
		Remember	Understand	Apply	Analyse	Evaluate	Create
Animal Acting(KS1-2 PE)	4-8 years	✓	✓				
Understanding Your Brain(KS2-4 Science)	8-18 years		✓	✓	✓		
Weather in the Garden(KS1-4 Art and Design)	6-18 years		✓	✓	✓		✓
My Three States as Sounds(KS2-4 Music)	8-18 years	✓	✓	✓			
The Boat on the River(KS3-4 Art and Design)	8-18 years		✓	✓	✓		✓
The Ladder(KS2-4 Art and Design)	8-18 years		✓	✓	✓		✓
Watching the States in Action(KS3-4 English)	11-18 years		✓	✓	✓	✓	
Naming My States	6-18 years	✓	✓	✓			

5. Next ask them to choose one animal for feeling like they want to run or fight or shout or scream or break things – explain that this might be an angry feeling. Ask them to draw the animal.
6. Finally, ask them to choose an animal for when they feel like they want to hide and not move and not speak – this is most likely a scared feeling. Again, ask them to draw the animal.
7. Recap by asking for volunteers to compare their three animals.

For young children, this activity is where you establish the three different states, but without using the terms 'ventral vagal', 'sympathetic mobilisation' and 'dorsal shutdown'. In future activities, when referring to the three states, use the animal metaphors as your descriptors, for instance, 'when you feel like a happy puppy/angry lion/hiding mouse'.

Understanding Your Brain

Objective: To identify different areas of the brain and their functions.
Context: Developing better sense of self-awareness by learning about how the brain works, and applying understanding to own feelings and behaviours.
Cross-curricular Links: KS2-4 Science.
Age range: 8-18 years.
Time: 20-30 minutes.
Resources: A simple unlabelled diagram of the human brain printed out for each pupil (examples can be easily found online), and visible on a whiteboard.
Activity
1. Start by asking pupils what they believe the function of the brain is.
2. Explain that the brain is part of the central nervous system (also containing the spinal cord and nerves) and that part of the central nervous system is the Autonomic Nervous System (ANS). Using your understanding from Part I of this book, explain that the ANS detects signs of safety and signs of threat below your level of awareness, and it controls which autonomic state you are in. At this point, you could explain that there are three autonomic states, but learning about those will be for another lesson. Explain that the ANS is connected to the most ancient part of the brain – the brainstem. Show the pupils where this is on your whiteboard diagram.
3. Hand out the diagrams and ask pupils to label the brainstem. You could then explain the other functions of the brainstem, which are focused on survival, e.g., controlling heart rate and digestion, etc. You could also explain that this is the only part of our brain that we share with reptiles, hence its alternative name – the reptilian brain. You may ask pupils to add these details to their own diagram of the brain.
4. Next show where the limbic system is (the mammalian brain) and what it is associated with, then the neocortex and its association with higher thinking and social engagement. You will be drawing on your own understanding from Chapter 1, so check that you are confident with your own knowledge before the lesson. Again, pupils could add labels and details to their diagram.
5. Finally, give some examples of different behaviours and ask pupils to identify which part of the brain would be predominantly responsible, e.g., feeling comforted when you

stroke your pet; figuring out a maths problem; your heart racing when you hear the fire alarm; telling a friend about a difficult problem; feeling angry when someone you trusted lied to you; feeling butterflies in your tummy when you have to speak in front of the whole class.

Weather in the Garden

Objective: To use art and metaphor to compare the three autonomic states.
Context: Developing understanding of their three autonomic states using creativity, and encouraging self-reflection.
Cross-curricular Links: KS1-4 Art and Design.
Age range: 6-18 years.
Time: 30-60 minutes.
Resources: Art materials (e.g., paints, pastels, pencils, collage materials, etc.).
Activity
1. Start with a recap of what the ANS is, if you have already covered it, or give a brief explanation of the purpose of the ANS.
2. Explain that we have three autonomic states, controlled by the ANS. Start by explaining the ventral vagal state, giving examples of how it feels and when we are most likely to be in this state. Explain that the next two states are our response to threat, starting with sympathetic mobilisation, then dorsal shutdown. Again, give examples of what the states might feel like. With younger children, refer back to the Animal Acting activity to remind them of their three animals.
3. Give pupils the following instructions for their artwork: to draw a simple line-drawing of a garden or nature scene or landscape on a page; split the picture into three vertical parts; create artwork based on each of the three states, showing the states as weather or seasons - one for each part of the picture. For instance, the first part might be ventral vagal, symbolised by the sun shining and lots of lush greenery, the second part might be sympathetic mobilisation with a dark storm, etc. (see Figure 8.1).
4. Pupils could volunteer to share their artwork with the class at the end, or you could do a silent walk-around where everyone sees everyone else's artwork, but the rule is that nobody is allowed to comment. This allows everyone to feel seen without fear of judgement.

My Three States as Sounds

Objective: To use sound as a creative means of identifying and comparing the three autonomic states.
Context: Developing understanding of their three autonomic states using creativity, and encouraging self-reflection.
Cross-curricular Links: KS2-4 Music.
Age range: 8-18 years.
Time: 30-40 minutes.

Figure 8.1 Example piece of artwork for 'Weather in the Garden' activity

Resources: YouTube or another extensive source of music for the whole class to listen to together, and possibly a selection of musical instruments.

Activity

1. Start with a recap of what the ANS is, if you have already covered it, or give a brief explanation of the purpose of the ANS.
2. Explain what the three autonomic states are and how they feel, starting with the ventral vagal state.
3. Discuss how we can use our senses to explore ways of understanding and representing the three states. Play a simple sound (for instance, a note on a musical instrument) or make a sound yourself using your voice that you feel represents the ventral vagal state well and ask the pupils to identify which state the sound best matches with. Repeat with sounds to represent the other two states.
4. Ask for volunteers to play or make sounds for different states, for the class to identify. You may want to discuss how sounds can feel different to different people, so everyone might not agree and there are no right or wrong answers.
5. Repeat using music from YouTube (or similar) and ask pupils to volunteer music they feel best represents the three states.
6. Ask pupils to make three lists of music to represent the three states for themselves.

The Boat on the River

Objective: To use art and metaphor to compare the three autonomic states.
Context: Developing understanding of their three autonomic states using creativity, and encouraging self-reflection.
Cross-curricular Links: KS3-4 Art and Design.
Age range: 8-18 years.
Time: 30-60 minutes.
Resources: Art materials (e.g., paints, pastels, pencils, collage materials, etc.).
Activity

1. Start with a recap of what the ANS is, if you have already covered it, or give a brief explanation of the purpose of the ANS. If you have completed the Weather in the Garden activity, you will need little explanation, as this is a similar activity.
2. Explain/recap what the three autonomic states are and how they feel, starting with the ventral vagal state.
3. Give pupils the following instructions for their artwork: to draw a simple river crossing the page from left to right; split the picture into three vertical parts; create artwork based on each of the three states, showing the states as a boat on the river - one for each part of the picture. I recommend the three states are arranged so the water flows *towards* the ventral vagal state. For instance, the first part as dorsal shutdown could be symbolised by boggy mud that the boat can barely move through, the second part might be sympathetic mobilisation with rapids and the boat being thrown around, and the third as ventral vagal could be smooth-flowing water (see Figure 8.2). Ask pupils to add words to go with each state - they don't have to be sentences, or even make sense to others, so long as they make sense to the pupil.
4. As in 'Weather in the Garden', pupils could volunteer to share their artwork with the class at the end, or you could do a silent walk-around.

The Ladder

Objective: To explore how autonomic states can be 'blended'.
Context: Developing understanding of their three autonomic states, extending to blended states, and encouraging self-reflection.
Cross-curricular Links: KS2-4 Art and Design.
Age range: 8-18 years.
Time: 20 minutes.
Resources: Colouring pencils.
Activity

1. Start with a recap of what the ANS is, and what the three autonomic states are and how they feel, referring to activities completed on this subject so far.
2. Ask pupil to draw a large ladder stretching from the top to the bottom of their page. Explain that at the bottom of the ladder is the dorsal shutdown state, then halfway up is sympathetic mobilisation and at the top is ventral vagal.

muddy marshes

smash

fast

mud

rocks

HELP!

stuck

slow   stopped

crashing scary cold

falling

warm

flowing relaxed easy

Figure 8.2 Example piece of artwork for 'The Boat on the River' activity

3. Ask pupils to choose a colour for each state, and shade in the three parts of the ladder. Then label each part with the name of the state and some words to describe how that state feels.

4. Explain that sometimes we can be in 'blended' states and give the two examples of: ventral vagal + sympathetic mobilisation, for instance, when playing sport; ventral vagal + dorsal shutdown, for instance, when extremely relaxed.

5. Ask pupils to draw a piece of rope tied between rungs on the ladder, connecting ventral vagal to sympathetic mobilisation and add their own examples (see Figure 8.3). They should be thinking of times when they feel mobilised and full of energy, yet safe and connected to their own body and to others. It may be helpful for pupils to work in pairs to discuss their ideas.

6. Repeat with the ventral vagal and dorsal shutdown connection. Pupils should be thinking of times they feel still, calm, and low in energy, but safe and connected to their own body and to others.

Ask for volunteers to offer their examples and reflect on how these blended states do not involve feeling overwhelmed by feelings – they feel safe and connected.

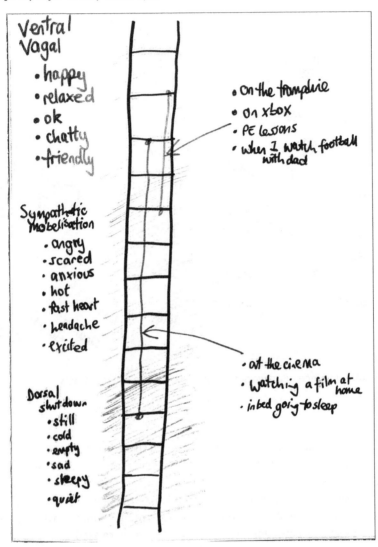

Figure 8.3 Example piece of artwork for 'The Ladder' activity

Watching the States in Action

Objective: To identify the three autonomic states and blended states in others.
Context: Consolidating learning about the three autonomic states, and practise identifying them.
Cross-curricular Links: KS3-4 English.
Age range: 11-18 years.
Time: 20-40 minutes.
Resources: Video clips from a popular film or programme that pupils will be familiar with. Choose more than one clip that clearly shows characters in each of the three autonomic states.

Activity

1. Start with a recap of what the ANS is, and what the three autonomic states are and how they feel, referring to activities completed on this subject so far.
2. Explain that you will be playing a video clip for everyone to watch and name a character to keep a close eye on. Once the clip has finished, ask pupils to discuss in pairs which autonomic state(s) they felt the character was in, then ask for contributions for a class discussion. Ask what observations they made that helped them decide. Remember there may be blended states, or separate states.
3. Repeat with further video clips.
4. As a reflective discussion at the end, explore how people can respond in different ways to their three states, but in every case, they are focused on either *connection* (ventral vagal) or *protection* (sympathetic mobilisation/dorsal shutdown).

Naming My States

Objective: To identify with the personal experience of the three autonomic states creatively.

Context: Encouraging self-reflection, consolidating understanding of the three autonomic states.

Age range: 6–18 years.

Time: 15–20 minutes.

Resources: None.

Activity

1. Remind pupils of the activities they have done so far in learning about their three autonomic states and reflecting on their experiences of them. They may want to look back in their books.
2. Ask pupils to split their page into three sections however they wish (vertically, horizontally or in more creative ways, such as three cloud shapes). For the first section, write down all the words associated with the ventral vagal state, from the activities they have done so far. Repeat for the other two sections to represent the other two states. This could also be done with simple drawings or symbols to represent words.
3. From the words they have written, ask pupils to choose one word from each section to be their 'name' for that state. For instance, ventral vagal state might be 'springtime', sympathetic mobilisation might be 'cymbals', and dorsal shutdown might be 'still'. They might want to underline or highlight their chosen words.
4. If time, ask pupils to share their words in pairs, small groups or with the class.

Section 4: Self-Awareness

In preparation for moving onto the activities focused on connecting with the body, pupils would benefit from practising self-awareness. The following activities apply the learning from the psychoeducation activities, encouraging pupils to become aware of and familiarise themselves with their own autonomic states, turning their focus inwards upon themselves (Table 8.3). Activities on self-awareness have the potential to be emotionally exposing, so please ensure your group has established sufficient emotional safety. If need be, revisit Section 2, 'Creating a Safe Space'.

I Feel Happy When ...

Objective: To identify and share positive feelings with others.

Context: Strengthening ventral vagal states of all involved, strengthening connection with others through activating social engagement, encouraging self-reflection.

Cross-curricular Links: KS1-2 English (Spoken English).

Age range: 4-18 years.

Time: 10 minutes (this could work well as a starter activity).

Resources: None (or a Talking Object if you have established one).

Activity

1. Ask pupils, one by one to finish the sentence 'I feel happy when ...', demonstrate by starting with yourself.

2. Alternatives could be 'I feel confident when ...', or 'I feel calm when ...', 'I feel proud when ...' etc., so variations of this activity could be used again and again.

Table 8.3 'Self-Awareness' activities mapped against Bloom's Taxonomy, with age range and cross-curricular links

Self-awareness activities	Age range	Bloom's Taxonomy					
		Remember	Understand	Apply	Analyse	Evaluate	Create
I Feel Happy When ...(KS1-2 English)	4-18 years	✓					
Word Cloud(KS2-4 English)	8-18 years	✓					
The Minister's Cat(KS2 Music)	8-18 years	✓					
Body Maps	8-18 years		✓	✓		✓	✓
Regulating Resources(KS2-4 Art and Design)	6-18 years				✓	✓	✓
The Tracker(KS3-4 Maths; KS3-4 Science)	11-18 years		✓	✓			✓
My Heartbeat(KS2-4 Science)	8-18 years		✓	✓	✓		
Feelings Charades(KS4 Drama)	6-18 years			✓		✓	✓
The Colours of My Feelings(KS1-4 Art and Design)	4-18 years			✓			✓
Trees of Words	4-18 years	✓					
Cartoon Strip(KS24 Art and Design)	10-18 years			✓	✓		✓

Word Cloud

Objective: To list 'feelings' words and display them creatively.

Context: Encouraging emotional literacy and self-awareness, strengthening connection with others through activating social engagement.

Cross-curricular Links: KS2-4 English.

Age range: 8-18 years.

Time: 20 minutes.

Resources: Access to the internet and a printer for pupils, in pairs.

Activity

1. Instruct pupils, working in pairs, to search for a free 'Word Cloud' generator website or give them the name of a website to use.
2. Ask pupils to name as many feelings words as they can, to create a word cloud, e.g., happy, sad, angry, scared, jealous, proud, lonely, loved, etc.
3. If possible, have the word clouds printed so they can be displayed or stuck into the pupils' books.
4. Reflect on the most obscure feelings words used and talk about their meanings, with examples, to ensure all the pupils understand these words.

The Minister's Cat

Objective: To reflect on an anxiety-provoking experience and to normalise feelings through sharing with group.

Context: Experiencing a blended state of ventral vagal and sympathetic mobilisation, through a group activity using rhythm to self-regulate anxiety, strengthening connection with others through activating social engagement.

Cross-curricular Links: KS2 Music.

Age range: 8-18 years.

Time: 30 minutes.

Resources: None.

Activity

1. If you are unfamiliar with 'The Minister's Cat' parlour game, it may be easiest to learn by watching a YouTube video of it being played before the lesson – you may find a number of variations but they all meet the objective of this activity. The game involves everyone clapping a simple rhythm, then the first person saying to the rhythm "The minister's cat is a ---- cat" where the missing word is an adjective starting with the letter A. The second person does the same, but using an adjective starting with B, and so on. Alternatively, you could abandon alphabetical order, and players could give any adjective, or follow a theme, e.g., colours or adjectives related to movement, all adjectives beginning with one letter, or silly themes such as vegetables or other animals – the minster's cat could be broccoli-cat or a rhinoceros-cat!
2. Start the game with a slow rhythm, then once everyone's confidence builds, let it speed up.

3. Once everyone has had two or more turns, stop the game, and ask pupils to volunteer how it felt to play the game. Did they feel nervous or anxious or excited when it was getting close to their turn? What could they feel in their body, e.g., raised heartrate, shakiness, hot? How did they feel once they'd had their turn? What could they feel in their body? Was the feeling different when it came round to their turn again?

4. Discuss how being able to keep the rhythm and know what to say meant they had their ventral vagal state online, but the body responses may indicate some sympathetic mobilisation *at the same time*, i.e., a blended state.

5. If there is time, ask pupil to write a reflection on the game in their books, focusing on what they felt in their body.

Body Maps

Objective: To reflect on how body sensations relate to emotional states.

Context: Encouraging self-reflection and developing self-awareness, normalising body responses to strong emotions through sharing with others, strengthening connection with others through activating social engagement.

Age range: 8-18 years.

Time: 20-30 minutes.

Resources: A simple body outline printed out, one for every pupil, coloured pens/pencils.

Activity

1. Reflect with pupils what they feel in their bodies with different strong emotions, such as anger, fear, excitement, relaxation, sadness, etc.

2. Hand out the body outline sheets and ask pupils to choose a colour for one of the emotions discussed and label the diagram with the body sensations that are associated with that emotion, e.g., for anger they might label hot head and shaking hands in the colour red. Point out that different people may have different body sensations.

3. Then pupils can choose another colour for another emotion and repeat the labelling. They might want to add a key to show which emotions are represented by which colours. These sheets could then be glued into their books.

4. If time, ask pupils to compare their body map with a partner's, to see how they are different and how they are the same.

Regulating Resources

Objective: To list self-regulating strategies.

Context: Encouraging self-reflection and developing self-awareness, developing capacity for self-regulation and planning for strengthening ventral vagal states.

Cross-curricular Links: KS2–4 Art and Design.

Age range: 6–18 years.

Time: 20 minutes.

Resources: None, maybe art materials.

Activity

1. Ask pupils to give suggestions of things they do to help themselves feel better if they feel overwhelmed by their feelings, for instance, if they are feeling angry, sad, worried, etc. Write any ideas on the board and add your own, so you are part of the discussion. You could also ask for things pupils do that maintain good feelings.
2. On a double page in their book or a large piece of paper, ask pupils to create a mindmap/list/artwork (or any other presentation) of all the strategies they have for self-regulating, and in pencil, any ideas they have gathered from the class that they would like to try out.
3. To finish ask each pupil to give one new idea they are going to try.

The Tracker

Objective: To use a chart to track autonomic states for a day or week.

Context: Encouraging self-reflection and developing self-awareness, to identify times of the day/week where self-regulation strategies could be introduced and patterns of changes in autonomic states.

Cross-curricular Links: KS3–4 Maths; KS3–4 Science.

Age range: 11–18 years.

Time: 20–30 minutes.

Resources: None.

Activity

1. In their book, ask pupils to draw simple graph axes. Split the y-axis into three parts, the bottom part labelled as dorsal shutdown, the middle part as sympathetic mobilisation and the top part as ventral vagal (Figure 8.4). It may be useful for pupils to use the names they chose for their states in the activity Naming my States. Along the x-axis, they could write hours starting around 7a.m. until the current time (if you are doing this activity early in the day, they could include half-hours).
2. Now ask them to mark on their chart where they were at the start of the day, in terms of their autonomic state, and to write a few words to say what was happening at that time. Blended states could be marked by shading an area or drawing a vertical line – there is no right or wrong way of doing this, remember, the purpose is to encourage self-reflection. Continue adding to the chart, joining the points and adding notes, so a line forms with a story for the day.
3. This activity could then be repeated tracking yesterday and/or tracking the week by writing days along the x-axis.
4. Ask pupils if they can identify any patterns, and if they have any ideas of strategies/activities they could introduce into their day/week to help.

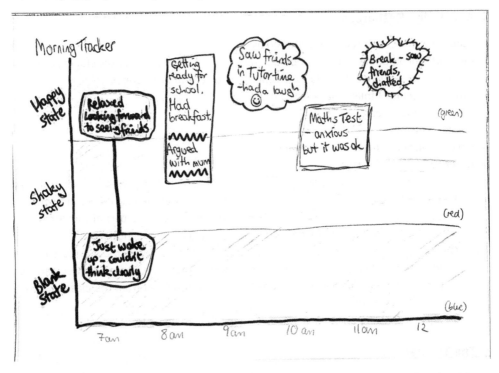

Figure 8.4 Example chart for 'The Tracker' activity

My Heartbeat

Objective: To feel the change in heartrate/pulse moving from ventral vagal to sympathetic mobilisation and back to ventral vagal. To list examples of the heartrate speeding up and slowing down.

Context: Encouraging body awareness, noticing body responses to sympathetic mobilisation, practising self-regulation through visualisation.

Cross-curricular Links: KS2-4 Science.

Age range: 8-18 years.

Time: 20 minutes.

Resources: A short video clip to show the whole class something that will make them jump - nothing too frightening!

Activity

1. Explain that we can feel our pulse in our neck (just under the jaw) or on our wrist and ask pupils to find their pulse. If pupils have a smart watch, ask them to use it to watch their heartrate.

2. Once pupils have found their heartrate/pulse, show them the short video clip, then as soon as it has finished ask them to notice what has happened to their heartrate/pulse - hopefully they will feedback that their heartrate increased.

3. Discuss why their heartrate increased in terms of their ANS moving them into sympathetic mobilisation because it detected a potential threat.

4. Now ask pupils to imagine the most relaxing place they can think of (they could close their eyes for this). Ask them to imagine what they can see and hear, what they feel on their skin, what they can smell, in this relaxing place. Give them a few moments to fully immerse themselves in their imagined relaxing place.

5. Now ask pupils to notice what has happened to their heartrate, and feedback. Ask if they can explain the change in their heartrate, in terms of the activity of their ANS.

6. In their book, ask pupils to draw up a table with two columns. As the heading for the first column, ask them to write 'My heart speeds up when ...' and in the second column, 'My heart slows down when ...', then ask them to make a list of experiences/feelings/activities, etc. Point out that there could be positives and negatives in each column, e.g., excitement and exercise can cause your heart to speed up, and extreme fear can cause your heart to slow down (i.e., dorsal shutdown). This is not about the positives and negatives; it is about developing body awareness.

Feelings Charades

Objective: To explore how different emotions feel and look.

Context: Encouraging self-reflection and developing self-awareness, strengthening connection with others through activating social engagement.

Cross-curricular Links: KS4 Drama.

Age range: 6-18 years.

Time: 20-30 minutes/

Resources: Small cards with names of different emotions, e.g., sad, happy, angry, confused, disgusted, bored, frightened, loving, excited, etc. For teenagers, you may want to include some more complex emotions, such as jealous, conflicted, isolated, vengeful, stressed, heartbroken, suspicious, etc. For younger children, you could use emoji pictures on the cards instead of words.

Activity

1. Split the class into small groups of 2-4 pupils.

2. Give each group a card, and a few minutes to prepare, then ask each group to mime/act the emotion on the card for the rest of the class to guess (the group performing are not allowed to speak). Point out that the pupils within a group may have different ways of acting the same emotion, which is fine because we all feel our emotions in our own way. Be aware that some pupils might find this game challenging and emotionally exposing as miming an emotion may connect them strongly with their own experience of that emotion, for instance, a lonely teenager miming 'isolated', or a bullied child miming 'frightened'. The cards do not have to be given out randomly, you can take control over which group has which card.

3. After the game, reflect on which emotions were easy/hard to mime and to guess, and why.

The Colour of My Feelings

Objective: Identify colours to associate with different emotions.

Context: Encouraging self-reflection and self-awareness, using creativity.

Cross-curricular Links: KS1–4 Art and Design.

Age range: 4–18 years

Time: 20–30 minutes.

Resources: Art materials. For young children, the book, *My Many Coloured Days*, by Dr Seuss (1996) would be helpful.

Activity

1. For younger children, start by reading them the book *My Many Coloured Days*. For older children and teenagers, discuss how colours are sometimes used to describe feelings such as 'feeling blue', 'seeing red', or 'green with envy'.

2. Ask pupils to give ideas of colours they feel represent certain feelings, pointing out that different people may choose different colours.

3. In their books, ask pupils to choose different colours for a number of feelings. They could create abstract art (painting/collage/shapes, etc.), based on the colours to represent each feeling, or simply colour in a box for each feeling, or write the feeling in the chosen colour. For very young children, you may want to just focus on the four core feelings – angry, sad, happy, and frightened. For older children and teenagers, you may want to ask them to choose any ten feelings.

Trees of Words

Objective: To create a group presentation with contributions from every person, based on self-reflection.

Context: Encouraging self-reflection and self-awareness, strengthening connection with others through contributing to a group creation, building self-esteem.

Age range: 4–18 years.

Time: 15 minutes.

Resources: A cut-out of a tree trunk and branches to be stuck on the wall, or twigs made into a small model tree. Small pieces of green paper cut into leaf shapes, enough for one per pupil.

Activity

1. This activity can come in many variations. This is a version focused on affirmations and building self-esteem. Give each pupil a leaf and ask them to write on it something they have done well this week. Then ask them to attach their leaf to the tree. You could do one yourself too. For very young children, they could paint their hand and make a handprint on the leaf, or paint the leaf with their favourite colour, or draw a simple picture or write their name on their leaf.

2. Pupils can then take a few moments, maybe a few pupils at a time, to look at other people's leaves. For emotional safety, it may be helpful to ask pupils not to make comments on what they read, similar to the silent walk-around.

3. Other variations of the Tree of Words: pupils writing something kind they have done that week on their leaf; pupils finish the statement 'I am proud of myself for ...', or 'I am a ... person' with a positive adjective about themselves, or 'I am a good friend because ...'; pupils writing their hopes or goals on the leaves, or a good memory from being in this class (good as a transition activity close to the end of the academic year). You could give the tree an appropriate name according to what the leaves say, for instance, 'The Tree of Friendship' or 'The Kindness Tree', etc.

Cartoon Strip

Objective: To explore new endings to stories of being overwhelmed by sympathetic mobilisation.

Context: Encouraging self-reflection and self-awareness, applying learning of autonomic states, normalising autonomic responses, strengthening connection with others through activating social engagement.

Cross-curricular Links: KS2-4 Art and Design.

Age range: 10-18 years.

Time: 30-50 minutes.

Resources: None, maybe some art materials.

Activity

1. Give an example to pupils about a time you felt your sympathetic mobilisation state activated and it seemed to take control of your actions. Choose an experience that is not highly emotional for yourself, and that you feel happy about sharing with your pupils. This is not about regret, but about applying new self-awareness and understanding of autonomic states – emphasise this point for the group discussion. By giving an experience of your own, you are modelling self-awareness and strengthening the safety of the group, but only do this if you do actually feel emotionally safe with the group. If you don't, then go back to Section 2, 'Creating a Safe Space', to see if there is an area that needs addressing. If *you* don't feel emotionally safe, your pupils probably don't either.
2. Talk through what you would have liked the ending of your experience of sympathetic mobilisation to have been. Relate your new ending to your learning about autonomic states. For instance, if you knew that your breathing was very fast at the time and you couldn't think clearly, you now know that was a sign that you were in sympathetic mobilisation, but in your new ending, you would focus on breathing slowly and distracting yourself with a thinking task such as counting or saying a helpful phrase, which could have helped you back to your ventral vagal state.
3. Ask pupils to volunteer any experiences they have had where they know their sympathetic mobilisation had taken control of their actions. You may want to remind the group of the rules around emotional safety. Ask how they would have liked their story to end.
4. In their books, ask pupils to draw gridlines to create boxes for a cartoon strip, then to tell their story as a cartoon, with the ending they would have liked, based on their knowledge of the autonomic states (see Figure 8.5).

Figure 8.5 Example story for the 'Cartoon Strip' activity

Section 5: Connecting to the Body

Now the pupils have had some practice turning their focus inwards and applying their understanding of their autonomic states to their own emotional experience, we move onto strengthening their ventral vagal state through deepening the mind-body connection (Table 8.4).

Breathing Exercises

Objective: To focus attention on the action and sensation of breathing.

Context: Encouraging and strengthening connection with the body, strengthening the ventral vagal state through regulating the breath.

Cross-curricular Links: KS2-4 Science.

Age range: 4-18 years.

Time: 5-10 minutes.

Resources: None.

Activity

1. This exercise would be best repeated at the start and/or end of longer activities, so it becomes more of a practice. There are different approaches to breathing exercises depending on the developmental age of the pupils. Start by explaining that everyone is going to be focusing on their breathing for a few minutes, as a group.
2. For younger children, explain that you are going to keep your breathing normal and notice the cool air as it comes in through your nose, and the warm air coming out through your nose. Then demonstrate for one breath. When you ask the children to

Table 8.4 'Connecting to the Body' activities mapped against Bloom's Taxonomy, with age range and cross-curricular links

Connecting to the Body activities	Age range	Bloom's Taxonomy					
		Remember	Understand	Apply	Analyse	Evaluate	Create
Breathing Exercises (KS2-4 Science)	4-18 years			✓			
Power Poses (KS1-2 PE; KS3-4 Drama)	4-18 years			✓		✓	✓
Clever Toes (KS1-2 PE)	4-18 years			✓		✓	
Sensations Mindfulness	11-18 years					✓	
Mindful Moving (KS1-2 PE)	4-10 years			✓		✓	✓
The Growing Seed (KS1-2 Science; KS1-2 PE)	4-10 years		✓	✓			✓
Marching to the Drum (KS1-2 Music)	4-10 years	✓		✓			
Musical Mimes (KS1-2 PE; KS1-2 Drama)	6-11 years			✓		✓	✓
It's Not a Stick, It's a ... (KS1-2 PE; KS3-4 Drama)	6-18 years					✓	✓
Obstacle Course (KS1-2 PE; KS3-4 Drama)	4-18 years			✓		✓	✓

try, don't be surprised if you get some very exaggerated breathing! Encourage normal breathing but remember this is about strengthening their connection with their body, so only correct them if you think they are not feeling that connection. With practice, they will find their way to normal breathing.

3.   With older children and teenagers, ask them to put one hand on their stomach and one on their chest and notice the movements as they breathe in and out. Explain that deep breathing involves movement of the diaphragm, which is a large flat muscle under the lungs, so deep breathing can be felt when the stomach moves in and out. Encourage pupils to take a long breath, counting slowly to four, and notice their stomach moving out. If they are able, ask them to hold their breath for a count of four, then breathe out for four and hold for four. This is known as Square Breathing and can be very effective for self-regulating and relaxing.

4.   You may want to ask pupils to write a list of the things they noticed in their body as they breathed, and any changes they noticed in their mind. Point out that they may have experienced unexpected changes, such as their shoulders or jaw relaxing or their thinking becoming clearer.

Power Poses

Objective: To experiment with body poses that increase confidence.

Context: Encouraging and strengthening connection with the body, strengthening the ventral vagal state, building confidence.

Cross-curricular Links: KS1-2 PE; KS3-4 Drama.

Age range: 4-18 years.

Time: 20-30 minutes

Resources: None.

Activity

1.   Start by explaining that how we are feeling can affect the body. For example, when we feel excited, it can be hard to sit still, or if we feel angry, our hands might go into fists or start shaking. You could ask pupils for their own examples of how their body reacts to different feelings. Explain that this can work in reverse – we can use our body to affect how we are feeling, for instance, slow breathing or using power poses.

2.   Demonstrate a power pose by standing in the superhero pose (feet to be shoulders-width apart, hands on hips, head held high). Ask the pupils what they think you might be feeling, standing in this pose.

3.   Now ask pupils to try it – make sure they stand tall and hold their heads high (and make sure they continue breathing as there can be a temptation to hold the breath).

4.   Demonstrate some other power poses for the pupils to try – arms raised like the winner of a race; one fist in the air and the other hand on the hip, with one foot stepping forward; one arm outstretched like Superman about to fly; Usain Bolt's trademark pose. Ask pupils if they can think of any power poses for everyone to try.

5.   You could also ask pupils to come up with affirmations to accompany each pose such as 'This is me!', 'Here I am!', 'I am the best!', 'I can do it!'

6. Reflect as a group how the power poses felt, and how it felt to say the affirmations. Reflect on when power poses could be useful, e.g., at the start of an exam day, and where would be a good place to do the power pose - as a group? Privately at home?
7. You may want to ask pupils to draw a picture in their book of the power pose they liked the most and their affirmation to go with it.

Clever Toes

Objective: To focus on and connect with one specific part of the body - the toes!
Context: Encouraging and strengthening connection with the body, strengthening the ventral vagal states of everyone through shared enjoyment.
Cross-curricular Links: KS1-2 PE.
Age range: 4-18 years.
Time: 10-20 minutes.
Resources: Various small items you might have in the room, or pupils might have with them, such as pens, keys, etc.
Activity
1. Explain that pupils will be picking up a selection of items using only their toes. They will be doing the activity in pairs. Ask them to take off their shoes, and ideally their socks too.
2. One person in the pair chooses five items for the other person to pick up from the floor and put onto a piece of paper on the floor nearby, using just their toes. Once they have achieved this, pupils in the pair swap roles. They may need to use both feet together and do the activity while sitting on their chair. If they find this easy, the game could be extended to picking up a pencil with their toes then writing their name with it.
3. As a group, reflect on how this game felt, and notice that they had to have their attention fully on their toes. As an extension, ask them to try focusing as fully as they can on a different part of the body which they could move about, for instance, their little finger or their tongue.

Sensations Mindfulness

Objective: To experience guided mindfulness.
Context: Encouraging and strengthening connection with the body, strengthening the ventral vagal state, practising mindfulness.
Age range: 11-18 years.
Time: 20 minutes.
Resources: None.
Activity
1. Explain to pupils that mindfulness is about being in the present moment and focusing on the senses, thereby feeling a strong connection to the body. Ask pupils to find a comfortable sitting position. It may be helpful to do the breathing exercise just before this activity.

2.   Ask pupils to close their eyes if they feel comfortable to do so, otherwise to find a spot ahead of them to rest their gaze on.

3.   Keeping your voice gentle and speaking slowly, ask pupils to bring their attention to the top of their head ... then their face ... then neck, encourage them to relax all the little muscles, as they move their attention to their shoulders. Continue down the body, including noticing the feeling of the chair beneath them, what they are touching with their hands and arms, and the feeling of the floor under their feet. Include noticing what they can hear and any smell in the air. Take your time guiding them through this and allow short silences as you speak. When you have come to the end, gently ask pupils to move their fingers and toes, then open their eyes, so they can reorient them-selves in the room.

4.   Reflect with the group how the experience was for them. For pupils who found this very relaxing and would like to try more in their own time, advise them on apps, such as Headspace or Calm, as resources for guided meditations, visualisations, and mind-fulness. Encourage pupils to reflect on how strong they feel their ventral vagal state is now the mindfulness is over, and how connected they feel with their body.

5.   As with the breathing exercise, this would be best repeated from time to time, so it becomes a practice. Once pupils can easily settle into mindfulness, if possible, take the practice outside so pupils have the added sensory experience of fresh air and nature.

Mindful Moving

Objective: To experience mindfulness through movement.
Context: Encouraging and strengthening connection with the body, strengthening the ventral vagal state through focus and using the imagination, practising mindfulness.
Cross-curricular Links: KS1-2 PE.
Age range: 4-10 years.
Time: 20 minutes.
Resources: None.
Activity

1.   Explain to pupils that they are going to focus on their body as they move around. Ask them to stand up and to imagine that the room is a quiet woodland with lots of trees, logs on the ground and lots of twigs and dried leaves like in Autumn. Their challenge is to creep through the woodland without being noticed, so they are going to have to walk very carefully to step over logs and not tread on the twigs or leaves.

2.   As the pupils walk slowly around the room, speak softly as you remind them of the task and the obstacles. Encourage pupils to notice each movement they make and to take it very slowly. You may like to add extra sensory details. For instance, maybe a cool breeze blows through the woods which makes everyone shiver, or there is a bird singing in the trees above so everyone looks up. Use your imagination and join in the actions, to help any pupils who might be struggling with the activity.

3.   As a group, reflect on how the activity felt and ask pupils what movements they made that they were paying close attention to.

The Growing Seed

Objective: To use the imagination to act out a seed growing into a plant.

Context: Encouraging and strengthening connection with the body, strengthening the ventral vagal state through using the imagination, introducing meditation.

Cross-curricular Links: KS1-2 Science; KS1-2 PE.

Age range: 4-10 years.

Time: 10-20 minutes.

Resources: None, although a time-lapse film of a seed growing into a plant may help at the start of the activity (there are plenty on YouTube).

Activity

1. Start by talking to the class about how seeds grow into plants, starting in the soil, growing a root and a shoot, then growing taller and growing leaves, etc. Also talk about what the seed/plant needs - water and sunlight. Show a time-lapse film of a seed growing if you have one.

2. Ask the children to find a space in the room and curl up into a tiny ball, to become a seed ready to grow.

3. Encourage pupils to imagine the sensory experience of being a seed in the soil where it feels warm, soft, and safe. Describe how the rain gently falls then the sun comes out and warms the earth, so the seed starts to grow. Keep your voice gentle and slow, allowing pauses, to encourage pupils to take it slow. Talk through the seed growing a shoot upwards through the soil until it reaches the sunlight, then its leaves opening. Explain that the child's face is the flower of the plant looking upwards towards the sun.

4. After the activity, pupils could draw a picture of the plant they became, including the flower that was their face.

Marching to the Drum

Objective: To move to the rhythm of a drum.

Context: Encouraging and strengthening connection with the body, strengthening the ventral vagal state through rhythm (hearing and moving to it).

Cross-curricular Links: KS1-2 Music.

Age range: 4-10 years.

Time: 10-15 minutes.

Resources: None, although a drum would be beneficial.

Acitivity

1. Ask the children to stand in a circle all facing to their right. Drum a slow rhythm on the desk or on a drum and ask pupils to march on the spot to the rhythm. Once the rhythm and movement of the group have been established, ask them to step forwards so everyone is marching to the beat of the drum together.

2. Vary the rhythm, making it faster, slower, louder, softer, and ask pupils to try to match their movement to the drum, for instance, they might tiptoe to a quieter beat. They could add in clapping or other body movements to the rhythm.

3. After the activity, ask pupils which autonomic state they thought they were in and why. Remind younger children of the Animal Acting activity used to identify the three states - ask them which *animal* they felt like when they were marching.

Musical Mimes

Objective: To mime/roleplay given actions to music.

Context: Encouraging and strengthening connection with the body, strengthening the ventral vagal state through focus and using the imagination.

Cross-curricular Links: KS1-2 PE; KS1-2 Drama.

Age range: 6-11 years.

Time: 10-20 minutes.

Resources: A source of music for the whole class to hear.

Activity

1. Explain that the pupils are going to be given an activity to mime while the music is playing, then when the music stops, they have to freeze. If anyone moves, they must sit down. Activities to mime could include cooking a meal, playing tennis (or another sport), tidying their room, shopping, washing the car, packing a suitcase ready to go on holiday, getting changed for PE, doing the washing-up, etc. You could change the action every time the music starts. Pupils who were out of the game early may become very impatient if you wait for the last person to win, so you may want to finish the game earlier.

2. After the game, ask pupils how it felt to focus on the activity and at the same time focus on listening for when the music stopped. Ask which autonomic state they thought they were in while playing the game, and how they could tell.

It's Not a Stick, It's a ...

Objective: To mime actions pretending a stick is something different.

Context: Encouraging and strengthening connection with the body, strengthening the ventral vagal state through focus, using the imagination, and connecting with others.

Cross-curricular Links: KS1-2 PE; KS3-4 Drama.

Age range: 6-18 years.

Time: 10-20 minutes.

Resources: A stick (any size). For young children, the book *Not a Stick*. by Antoinette Portis (2009) would be helpful.

Activity

1. Start by showing the pupils the stick, then mime the stick being something else, such as a toothbrush, umbrella, paintbrush, flute, etc. and ask the pupils to guess what the stick is now. For younger children you could read them the book, *Not a Stick*, or watch the YouTube animation of the book.

2. Ask if anyone has an idea for the stick and ask them to mime their idea with the stick for the class to guess. For younger children you could use the phrase 'It's not a stick it's a ...' for them to give their guess.

3. Reflect on how the game felt and what parts of their body they had to focus on when they were miming with the stick.

Obstacle Course

Objective: To move imaginatively through/over obstacles.

Context: Encouraging and strengthening connection with the body, strengthening the ventral vagal state through focus and using the imagination.

Cross-curricular Links: KS1-2 PE; KS3-4 Drama.

Age range: 4-18 years.

Time: 10-30 minutes.

Resources: None.

Activity

1. This activity follows a similar idea to the book/game 'We're Going on a Bear Hunt' as pupils will encounter obstacles to overcome on a long journey. A large space will need to be cleared in the middle of the room, or the group could be moved to a larger room (or even outside). Explain that they are going on an adventure with lots of obstacles to overcome, which they will act out.

2. Ask pupils to find a space and describe the obstacles one at a time for them to act their way through. Obstacles could include: swimming across a fast-flowing river; walking through a muddy sticky bog; crossing a very busy road; climbing a steep mountain in hail and snow; crossing a hot dry desert; walking through a haunted graveyard at night; crawling under a prickly hedge; crossing an ocean in a small boat in a storm; escaping from a hungry tiger. When they get to the end of their journey, tell them they need to dig and dig, then tell them they have found a treasure chest, which they can open to find the treasure they have always wanted!

3. With older pupils, you could reflect with the group on what happened in the autonomic states, as they may have experienced blended sympathetic mobilisation with ventral vagal activation as they acted some of the more frightening scenarios such as the haunted graveyard.

Section 6: Connecting to Others

The ventral vagal state can be strengthened through two types of connection: the connection between mind and body, and the connection with others (social engagement). The activities in this section focus on pupils sharing their experience and building their sense of togetherness as a group (see Table 8.5). Some of the activities are quite short so could be used before a longer activity from a different section.

Simon Says

Objective: To play the game 'Simon Says' as a group.
Context: Encouraging and strengthening connection with others, strengthening the ventral vagal state through focus, using the imagination, and connecting with others.
Cross-curricular Links: KS1-2 PE.
Age range: 4-11 years.
Time: 10-20 minutes.
Resources: None.
Activity
1. Ask all the pupils to stand up. Explain that they should follow any instruction you give that starts with 'Simon says ...', but not the instructions that don't start with 'Simon says ...'. If anyone breaks the rules of the game, they must sit down. Have a trial run with a couple of easy instructions (e.g., 'Simon says touch your toes' or 'Simon says stand on one foot'), so you know everyone understands the rules.
2. This game can be taken a little further to involve interactions, such as 'Simon says shake hands with the person next to you', 'Simon says give someone a high-five', 'Simon says link arms with two other people'.

Table 8.5 'Connecting to Others' activities mapped against Bloom's Taxonomy, with age range and cross-curricular links

Connecting to Others activities	Age range	Remember	Understand	Apply	Analyse	Evaluate	Create
Simon Says (KS1-2 PE)	4-11 years	✓	✓	✓		✓	
Handclapping Games (KS2 PE)	8-18 years	✓		✓		✓	
Mirror-Me (KS1-2 PE; KS3-4 Drama)	4-18 years			✓		✓	✓
Throwing Slime	6-11 years					✓	✓
My Favourite ...	4-18 years	✓				✓	
Spread the Smile (KS3-4 Drama)	6-18 years					✓	
One-Word Story (KS1-4 English)	6-18 years	✓		✓			✓
Pass the Squeeze	6-11 years					✓	
Charades (KS2 PE; KS3-4 Drama)	8-18 years					✓	✓
Body Building (KS2 PE; KS3-4 Drama)	8-18 years					✓	✓
Parachutes (KS1 PE)	4-6 years						✓

3. Reflect with the class on the connections they were making during the game – connecting with you by paying close attention to what you were saying, connecting with their own body and with others when following instructions.

Handclapping Games

Objective: To experience playing a handclapping game with another person.
Context: Encouraging and strengthening connection with others, strengthening the ventral vagal state through using rhythm and having fun with another person.
Cross-curricular Links: KS2 PE.
Age range: 8–18 years.
Time: 20–30 minutes.
Resources: Internet access for pupils, in pairs.
Activity

1. Ask if any of the pupils know any handclapping games that they would like to demonstrate to the class (e.g., 'pat-a-cake', or 'A Sailor went to Sea ...'). Explain that they are going to learn a new handclapping game with a partner.
2. Ask pupils to search the internet, in pairs, for a handclapping game they haven't tried before, and then try to learn it. Suggest they start very slow and build up speed as they get the hang of it.
3. Once everyone has found a game and practised it, ask if any pairs would like to demonstrate their handclapping game to the class.
4. Reflect with the class the importance of working together to learn the game and having to keep the same rhythm. Ask pupils to reflect on what autonomic state they felt they were in while learning the game, and then when performing it to the class.

Mirror-Me

Objective: To mirror another person's movements and facial expressions.
Context: Encouraging and strengthening connection with others, strengthening the ventral vagal state.
Cross-curricular Links: KS1-2 PE; KS3-4 Drama.
Age range: 4–18 years.
Time: 10–20 minutes.
Resources: None.
Activity

1. Explain that pupils are going to split into pairs, and that one person is going to be the mirror to the other person. They must mirror any body movements or facial expressions they see in the other person. They will have five minutes, then the pupils are to swap roles. For older children and teenagers, you could encourage dramatic movements and expressions, or even very subtle ones. Ask pupils to end with a smile.
2. For older pupils, you could explain the role of mirror neurones (see Chapter 6) and reflect on how the person being the mirror might have felt the same as the person they were mirroring. You could then go on to explain how our ANS all talk to each other all the time, and often we 'mirror' other people without even realising it.

Throwing Slime

Objective: To pretend to throw and catch slime in a group.
Context: Encouraging and strengthening connection with others, strengthening the ventral vagal state through using the imagination and having fun as a group.
Age range: 6-11 years.
Time: 10 minutes.
Resources: None.
Activity

1. Explain that you are going to throw imaginary slime to one of the pupils. They might catch it in their hands, or it might splat on their face. Ask them to use their imagination to act out what happens with the slime, then they can throw it to another pupil in the circle. Before you throw the slime, you might want to describe it, and ask pupils to contribute - its colour, texture, stickiness, temperature, etc. This will help spark their imaginations ready for catching and throwing the slime.
2. You could ask pupils to discuss or write about how they imagined the slime when they caught and threw it, and how it felt to watch other people acting with the slime.

My Favourite ...

Objective: To contribute to group, to get to know each other better.
Context: Encouraging and strengthening connection with others, strengthening the ventral vagal state.
Age range: 4-18 years.
Time: 10 minutes.
Resources: None.
Activity

1. With pupils sitting in a circle ask them in turn to give their favourite animal/food/toy/celebrity/music/hobby - any criteria you feel fits your class well. This helps with a new class of pupils who don't know each other well yet and helps everyone feel they are part of the group. The activity could be extended to giving the first letter of their answer for everyone else to guess, or a cryptic clue to their answer, or the sound of their chosen animal.
2. Reflect with pupils how it felt to find out this new information about group members and how it felt to share with the group.

Spread the Smile

Objective: To pass a smile or laugh around the group.

Context: Encouraging and strengthening connection with others, strengthening the ventral vagal state through having fun as a group.

Cross-curricular Links: KS3-4 Drama.

Age range: 6-18 years.

Time: 10 minutes.

Resources: None.

Activity

1. With pupils sitting in a circle, ask them to try to make their faces serious, and explain that you are going to smile at one pupil who should smile back then turn to smile at another pupil until everyone is smiling. The challenge is to *not* smile until someone smiles at you!

2. You could then extend the game to laughing with the smile and see how many pupils can stop themselves from laughing when it's not their turn yet!

3. Ask pupils to reflect on how the activity felt, and on how powerful smiling at someone can be. You could set them the challenge of seeing how many smiles they can cause today!

One-Word Story

Objective: To create a story with each person contributing one word at a time.

Context: Encouraging and strengthening connection with others, strengthening the ventral vagal state through using the imagination and having fun as a group.

Cross-curricular Links: KS1-4 English.

Age range: 6-18 years.

Time: 10-20 minutes.

Resources: None.

Activity

1. Explain that pupils are going to be making a story as a group, with each person only saying one word at a time. You give the first word, then each pupil has their turn. With younger children, you might find it easier to let them have a whole sentence rather than one word.

2. Reflect with the class on how everyone had to pay close attention to what had been said before and nobody had control over the story, as everyone was making the same size contribution.

Pass the Squeeze

Objective: To pass a hand signal around the group.
Context: Encouraging and strengthening connection with others, strengthening the ventral vagal state.
Age range: 6-11 years.
Time: 10 minutes.
Resources: None.
Activity

1. Arrange pupils to be standing or sitting in a circle (including you) all holding hands. Explain that you are going to squeeze the hand of the person next to you and when they feel it, they squeeze the hand of the next person and so on until it comes back to you. You could then change the hand signal to tapping your thumb on their hand, or another movement. Alternatively, the pupils could link little fingers and then squeeze their finger. Or with pupils not holding hands, they could pass around a high five or fist bump.

2. Reflect on how everyone is an important part of the circle, because if anyone let go, the whole game would stop.

Charades

Objective: To act out a given activity as a group.
Context: Encouraging and strengthening connection with others, strengthening the ventral vagal state through using the imagination and having fun as a group, building confidence.
Cross-curricular Links: KS2 PE; KS3-4 Drama.
Age range: 8-18 years.
Time: 30-40 minutes.
Resources: None.
Activity

1. Split the class into groups of 3-4 pupils and explain that you are going to give each group something to mime for the rest of the class to guess.

2. You could choose from categories such as films, TV programmes, day-to-day activities (e.g., shopping, making dinner, doing homework, making the bed, etc.), computer games, etc. Give them 5 minutes to plan what they are going to do before the performances for the class.

3. Reflect with the class how they worked together as a group. You could ask them to write about what skills they feel are needed for good groupwork and what they think they did well as a group.

Body Building

Objective: To use each person in the group to represent a given structure.
Context: Encouraging and strengthening connection with others, strengthening the ventral vagal state through using the imagination and having fun as a group.

Cross-curricular Links: KS2 PE; KS3-4 Drama.
Age range: 8-18 years.
Time: 30-40 minutes.
Resources: None.
Activity

1. Split the class into groups of 4-5 pupils and explain that you are going to give each group something to build themselves into, using their bodies, for the rest of the class to guess. They are allowed to have moving parts, but they are not allowed to make any sounds.
2. Ideas for structures/objects could be a bridge, a fence with a gate, a tree, a car, a picnic bench, a ladder, a bus shelter, etc. Give them 5-10 minutes to plan what they are going to do before performing for the class.
3. Reflect with the class how they worked together in their groups and how they had to be well connected to their own body.

Parachutes

Objective: To play with the parachute as a group.
Context: Encouraging and strengthening connection with others, strengthening the ventral vagal state through having fun as a group.
Cross-curricular Links: KS1 PE.
Age range: 4-6 years.
Time: 10-30 minutes.
Resources: A parachute and a large space.
Activity

There are many parachute games, which you may already know, or you can find plenty on the internet. Here are a few to get started. After the games, ask the children to name any of their feelings and what they noticed happening in their body. You will need the children standing spread out around the parachute, holding its edge, to start.

1. Identify two children on opposite sides who are going to high five under the parachute. On the count of three, everyone lifts the parachute above their heads, the two children run in underneath, high five, then run back to their places. Repeat with different pairs of children.
2. The children sit down holding the parachute edge in front of them. You choose two children on opposite sides who have the task of crawling under the parachute to swap places. As soon as the children are crawling, everyone lifts and shakes the parachute to make waves. The challenge is for the crawling children to make it to the right place. Repeat with different pairs of children.
3. All the children crouch down holding the parachute above their heads, then on the count of three, they step forward, pulling the parachute edge down behind them and sit on it, so they are all under the parachute. Choose one person to stand in the middle to be the 'tent pole' - this role could be swapped for other children.

After the activities, you could reflect with the children on what they found most fun and why.

Section 7: Self-Soothing

This section is focused on helping pupils discover ways to spend more time in their ventral vagal state, and plan for times when they might feel dysregulated. Pupil are encouraged to experiment with new strategies for self-regulation and build their own personal toolbox of resources (see Table 8.6).

Nature Walk

Objective: To connect with nature as a group.
Context: Strengthening the ventral vagal state through connection with nature.
Cross-curricular Links: KS1-2 Science.
Age range: 4-8 years.
Time: 10-30 minutes.
Resources: An outside area where there are plants, grass, trees, a beach, etc.
Activity
1. Take the children outside for a simple walk, in nature. There are various ways of doing a nature walk. You could ask children to walk in pairs and point out anything interesting they see to their partner, or they could walk quietly as you guide them to notice what is around them using all their senses (what they see, hear, smell, feel on their skin, taste in the air, etc.). You could ask them to walk in silence only paying attention to what they hear, then after a few minutes stop the group and ask the children to feedback what they heard on the walk. The purpose is for the children to experience strong ventral vagal states, so plan the walk using your knowledge of your pupils.
2. After the walk, pupils might write or draw something they heard/saw, etc., and write about what the walk felt like, using 'feelings words'. Pupils could make a list of times they can be in nature (for instance, playing in the garden after school, walking the dog, etc.).

Table 8.6 'Self-Soothing' activities mapped against Bloom's Taxonomy, with age range and cross-curricular links

Self-Soothing activities	Age range	Bloom's Taxonomy					
		Remember	Understand	Apply	Analyse	Evaluate	Create
Nature Walk(KS1-2 Science)	4-8 years	✓					
Helpful Apps	11-18 years				✓	✓	
Peaceful Place(KS2-4 Art and Design)	8-18 years						✓
Musical Stories(KS1-4 Music)	6-18 years				✓	✓	✓
Relaxing Music Review(KS3-4 Music)	11-18 years			✓	✓		
Singalong(KS2-3 Music)	8-14 years			✓	✓		
Fidget/Sensory Toys Circus	4-11 years				✓	✓	
Sensory Focus(KS2-4 Art and Design)	8-18 years					✓	✓
Guided Visualisation	8-18 years					✓	
Self-Soothing for Me	8-18 years			✓		✓	✓

Helpful Apps

Objective: To try out and review emotional wellbeing apps.
Context: Planning strategies for self-regulating and strengthening the ventral vagal state.
Age range: 11-18 years.
Time: 20-30 minutes.
Resources: Pupils will need to use their smart phones if they have them or have access to devices which apps can be downloaded onto.
Activity
1. Split the class into groups of 3-4. If anyone in the group has an emotional wellbeing app on their phone, ask them to tell the rest of the group about the app. Pupils can research emotional wellbeing apps either on their phones or a school device. Ask pupils to draw up a table in their book of pros and cons for each app they discuss.
2. Ask groups to feedback to the class which apps they have researched and discussed. Reflect on which apps are most popular and when pupils might find apps such as these most helpful to use.

Peaceful Place

Objective: To experience a visualisation of a peaceful place, and to anchor the feelings of safety and peace.
Context: Planning for self-regulating and strengthening the ventral vagal state through visualisation and creativity.
Cross-curricular Links: KS2-4 Art and Design.
Age range: 8-18 years.
Time: 20-50 minutes.
Resources: Art materials.
Activity
1. Explain to pupils that they are going to use their imagination to create a peaceful place, that will always be with them in their minds as a place they can go, to feel calm and safe.
2. Ask pupils to find a comfortable sitting position. It may be helpful to do the breathing exercise just before this activity. Ask pupils to close their eyes if they feel comfortable to do so, otherwise to find a spot ahead of them to rest their gaze on.
3. Keeping your voice gentle and speaking slowly, ask them to think of a place where they can feel most calm and relaxed. It might be a place they know well, like their bedroom, or an outside place, maybe somewhere they went on holiday, or it could be a completely made-up place, somewhere in the world they have never been, or a make-believe place, or a place they've seen in a film. It could be anywhere, so long as it's a place that makes them feel safe and peaceful.
4. Ask pupils to look around in their mind's eye at their peaceful place and notice everything they see. Ask them to look down at what is on the ground or floor, to look upwards, and to look behind them. Ask them to notice the colours, and to reach out and touch things to find out their textures. Ask them to notice what they can hear and what the air feels like – is it warm? Cold? Is there a breeze? What can they smell? Is

there anything in their place that they can taste, maybe there is food there. Use *all* the senses.

5. If the pupils are immersed in their visualisation, you could encourage them to imagine moving around in their peaceful place, to maybe go for a short walk and sit down somewhere, then to notice if anything is happening. Another extension to this activity could be to ask if there is anyone else there, or any animals, maybe a beloved pet, or interesting wildlife. If your pupils find it difficult to stay in the visualisation for long, you could split this activity over a few lessons, adding more detail to their peaceful place each time. When you have come to the end, gently ask pupils to move their fingers and toes, then to open their eyes, so they can reorient themselves in the room.

6. After the visualisation, ask pupils to create a piece of artwork of their peaceful place. Reassure them that their artwork may not look exactly like the picture in their mind and that's OK - it's about having a reminder of their peaceful place. They may want to give their peaceful place a special name. If you split this activity over a few lessons, encourage them to add to their artwork as they discover more details. A longer project for the artwork could be to create a diorama of the peaceful place over a few lessons.

7. Discuss with pupils that they can visit their peaceful place whenever they need to, and it might evolve with time. Remind them that they have complete control over their peaceful place, and they can change it whenever they like.

Musical Stories

Objective: To create a story or scene based on a piece of music.
Context: Strengthening the ventral vagal state through visualisation and creativity.
Cross-curricular Links: KS1-4 Music.
Age range: 6-18 years.
Time: 10-30 minutes.
Resources: Classical or instrumental music for the class to listen to, such as Clair de Lune by Debussy, Bolero by Ravel (starting about halfway through), The Lark Ascending by Vaughan Williams (the first half), Fanfare for the Common Man by Copland. It would be best to choose something they are unlikely to have heard before, so they don't already have a story associated with the music.

Activity

1. Explain to pupils that they are going to listen to a short piece of music and let their imagination create a story or picture from the music.
2. Ask pupils to find a comfortable sitting position. It may be helpful to do the breathing exercise just before this activity. Ask pupils to close their eyes if they feel comfortable to do so, otherwise to find a spot ahead of them to rest their gaze on.
3. Play the piece of music then once it is finished, ask pupils to volunteer their stories or pictures. Ask how the music and their story made them feel. This could be repeated with a second contrasting piece of music.
4. Reflect on how music can influence how we feel and be used as a source of creativity. As an extension, pupils could create a piece of artwork based on their story/picture.

Relaxing Music Review

Objective: To create a playlist of relaxing music.

Context: Planning for self-regulating and strengthening the ventral vagal state through listening to music.

Cross-curricular Links: KS3-4 Music

Age range: 11-18 years.

Time: 20-40 minutes.

Resources: Pupils will need to use their smart phones or devices they listen to music on if they have them or have access to devices on which they can listen to music.

Activity

1. Ask pupils to volunteer suggestions of music they find relaxing, and tell when they like to listen to relaxing music. You may need to point out that people have different tastes and it's OK for different people to find different music relaxing.
2. Ask pupils to listen to some music from the suggestions, that they haven't listened to before and to notice how the music makes them feel. Then ask pupils to create a personal playlist of relaxing music. An extension to this activity could be to create further playlists of uplifting music, energising music, music to work to, music that makes you want to dance/move, music that makes you want to sing along, etc.
3. Reflect with pupils how music can influence our autonomic states, and ask pupils to identify which music/playlist would help them move into a mobilised state if they were feeling shutdown, and which music/playlist would strengthen their ventral vagal state, etc.

Singalong

Objective: To sing along to music in a group.

Context: Strengthening the ventral vagal state and strengthening connection with others through singing in a group, and shared enjoyment in a group.

Cross-curricular Links: KS2-3 Music.

Age range: 8-14 years.

Time: 10-30 minutes.

Resources: A prepared playlist of music - it may be helpful to involve pupils in creating the playlist prior to the lesson, as you really need music the pupils will want to sing to (music from Disney films often goes down well!).

Activity

1. Explain to pupils that you are going to play some music for everyone to sing along to, but anyone who doesn't want to sing doesn't have to. It may be helpful to have a few percussion instruments available to add to the experience and to allow pupils who don't want to sing to still be involved.
2. If pupils are a little nervous about being heard, play the music loud. Join in yourself and encourage pupils to stand up and move to the music once they get into singing.
3. After the activity, reflect with pupils how it felt to be singing as a group, and which autonomic state they thought they were in. Explore opportunities for pupils to sing in groups, such as outside at lunchtime, school clubs and choirs, etc.

Fidget/Sensory Toys Circus

Objective: To experiment with and rate different fidget/sensory toys.

Context: Planning for self-regulating and strengthening the ventral vagal state through sensory experience.

Age range: 4-11 years.

Time: 20-50 minutes.

Resources: A selection of fidget toys and sensory toys if you have them, or items which could be effective alternatives for fidgeting with or providing a sensory experience, for instance, stationery (paperclips/Blu Tack/rubber bands), small pieces of fabric, a balloon filled with flour, buttons on a piece of string.

Activity

1. Ask pupils what fidget toys or sensory toys they have and in what ways they find them useful.
2. Arrange the items and toys around the room in 'stations' and split the pupils into groups of 2-3, so they can visit each station in turn trying out each toy (you will need at least as many stations as you have groups).
3. Before visiting the stations, ask pupils to make a table in their books where they can rate each toy. You could ask them to write positive and negative points about each toy, or give it scores out of ten in different categories (e.g., ease of carrying it around/cost/distracting noise/visual appeal/effectiveness at calming/messiness). Younger children could draw each toy and give it a number of ticks or crosses to show how much they liked or disliked it.
4. At each station, pupils can play with the toy and complete their rating. Give them about 2-3 minutes at each station, then move everyone on at the same time.
5. Once everyone has tried every toy, ask pupils to use their ratings to decide which toy was their favourite.
6. Discuss with the pupils what makes a good sensory/fidget toy and when are good times to use them. Point out that some people don't find sensory toys or fidget toys useful at all. Distinguish between using sensory/fidget toys for calming and using them for other reasons such as because they are fashionable, out of boredom or to draw attention from other people.

Sensory Focus

Objective: To create a list of soothing sensory input.

Context: Planning for self-regulating and strengthening the ventral vagal state through sensory experience.

Cross-curricular Links: KS2-4 Art and Design.

Age range: 8-18 years.

Time: 20-30 minutes.

Resources: None, maybe art materials.

Activity

1. Ask pupils to consider all their senses (sight, hearing, smell, taste, and touch) and to volunteer examples of sensory input they find most soothing. If they are slow to

volunteer ideas, start by giving some of your own ideas. Make sure you cover every sense. For instance, seeing the sunrise, hearing a cat purring, smelling lavender, tasting hot chocolate, touching warm water in the bath.

2. Ask pupils to make a mindmap or word cloud or piece of artwork (drawings/collage) or list of all the sensory input they find soothing or calming.
3. As an extension, pupils could write a plan for a soothing evening using ideas from their list, for instance, a warm bath with lavender scented bubble bath, then a hot chocolate whilst listening to relaxing music and snuggling with their cat.

Guided Visualisation

Objective: To listen to and reflect on a guided visualisation.
Context: Planning for self-regulating and strengthening the ventral vagal state through guided visualisation.
Age range: 8–18 years.
Time: 10–30 minutes.
Resources: A guided visualisation from a wellbeing app (e.g., Headspace or Calm) or on YouTube to be played to the class. Make sure you listen to it first to judge its suitability for your class.
Activity

1. Explain to pupils that they are going to listen to a recorded guided visualisation. Let them know where you found the visualisation you are going to play.
2. Ask pupils to find a comfortable sitting position. It may be helpful to do the breathing exercise just before this activity. Ask pupils to close their eyes if they feel comfortable to do so, otherwise to find a spot ahead of them to rest their gaze on (or some visualisations have visual component that pupils could watch, while listening).
3. Play the guided visualisation. It should end by bringing them back to the present, but if it hasn't, gently ask pupils to move their fingers and toes, then to open their eyes, so they can reorient themselves in the room.
4. Reflect with the class on how the visualisation felt. Discuss where recorded visualisations can be found and state that it is worth trying a few as the different voices reading the visualisation can feel different.
5. If there is time, pupils could research different websites and apps that have recorded visualisations and try listening to short extracts from a few to explore what appeals to them most.

Self-Soothing for Me

Objective: To plan grounding and self-regulating activities.

Context: Planning for self-regulating and strengthening the ventral vagal state.

Age range: 8-18 years.

Time: 30-40 minutes.

Resources: Art materials, card, scissors, treasury tags, depending on the creative activity chosen.

Activity

1. Explain to pupils that they are going to create a resource of personal strategies that they can use at times when they feel overwhelmed by their feelings. You could ask them to focus on strategies that involve others (friends, family, pets), i.e., co-regulation, or strategies without involving others, i.e., self-regulation. You may like to do this activity in two separate lessons, to cover both self-regulation and co-regulation.

2. Using the ideas gathered from the activities completed so far, ask pupils to make a list of their own strategies. They may like to look back in their books at the activities completed. They can then make flashcards of their strategies (which could be connected with a treasury tag) or make a spinner (a piece of card split into segments, with a pencil pushed through the middle), or a pocket-size booklet, or any other idea you have for presenting their ideas.

3. Reflect with the pupils on when they might need to use their collection of strategies, and how to make it most accessible.

Section 8: The Connection Diet

Identify a pupil you know who struggles with self-regulation, has a poor connection with their own body, struggles to connect well with other people and seems to spend more time at the Protection end of the Connection-Protection scale than the Connection end. This child may need extra help in finding and familiarising themselves with their ventral vagal state. Remember both connection with the body and connection with others (social engagement) strengthen the ventral vagal state.

Dan Hughes, as part of his attachment-focused therapy treatment for traumatised children, suggests an attitude to foster safety and trust, known by the acronym, PACE:

P = *Playfulness* - keeping your approach light and sharing fun together can help an emotionally challenged child relax and connect with you. This doesn't mean trying to be funny when the child is feeling sad or angry, but it does mean helping the child experience positive feelings, fun and enjoyment when they are able.

A = *Acceptance* - meeting the child where they are and accepting their feelings, thoughts, wishes and needs without judgement helps the child feel safe. This doesn't mean accepting all behaviours, as clear strong boundaries are also needed for safety, but the *emotions* driving those behaviours can be recognised and accepted.

C = *Curiosity* - showing interest in the child and attempting to understand what is happening in their emotional world. It doesn't mean making interpretations or naming a child's feeling for them, but it does mean wondering aloud about what the child might be feeling or thinking, which gives the message that you want to understand the child.

E = *Empathy* - showing compassion for the child's emotional world, by giving messages that you are interested and want to understand, and that the child is not alone. Not to be confused with sympathy, where we try to make things better. Empathy is about accepting someone else's challenging feelings and acknowledging those feelings. Brene Brown gives an excellent explanation of the difference between empathy and sympathy in a short, animated video - search 'Brene Brown Empathy' on YouTube.

As further reading, I would recommend *Belonging: A Relationship-based Approach for Trauma-informed Education* (Hughes, Phillips and Melim, 2020) which explores the use of Dyadic Developmental Psychotherapy (DDP), underpinned by PACE, in supporting traumatised children in school settings.

Before your time with the child you have identified for a Connection Diet programme, remind yourself of PACE, and consciously get yourself into the PACE mindset. Try to avoid coming into the child's special time feeling distracted, frustrated, impatient, etc. as such emotional states will interfere considerably with your PACE mindset, and will disrupt your connection with the child.

Most of the activities given in this section involve both you and the child doing things together and involve good eye-contact and non-verbal communication. The eye-contact and mirrored actions encourage the activation of mirror neurones, as mentioned in Chapter 6. The child benefits from your actions as your neurones associated with the action fire and their mirror neurones then also fire. Keep this in mind when you are doing the activities, especially where breathing and relaxing muscles are involved - the more you immerse yourself into the activity, the more the child or young person benefits. It should be noted that eye-contact for an autistic child or severely traumatised child can feel uncomfortable or even threatening, so gauge their response carefully and adjust accordingly. You might find you need to limit the eye-contact initially and build it in slowly as they start to feel safer with you.

The Connection Diet is so named as I wanted to emphasise that it is something needed *daily*, just as with a nutritional diet. My recommendation for this programme would be ten minutes every school day, ideally at the same time each day so the pupil knows when to expect this special time. I would recommend guiding the pupil's parents/carers to provide ten minutes doing similar activities on non-school days, close to the time of day you are doing them in school. Choose a time that is convenient for you and fits in to the rest of the day, for instance, the end of the day, the start of the day, or maybe just before or after lunch.

It is important that these activities are 1:1. If you have two children in need of this programme, give them different times or different adults to work with. If you try following the programme with both children together, you are likely to evoke competitive feelings and attention-seeking behaviours akin to sibling rivalry, which could sabotage your attempts to strengthen their ventral vagal states. Also, the activities chosen should be specifically for the pupil you are planning for, not as a compromise between two or more pupils.

Some of the activities with younger children do suggest physical contact, which I would describe as 'safe touch'. Brain development of infants requires safe touch from adults and for some children who have experienced developmental trauma, this may well have been lacking. Safe touch can be used to help repair some of the early disruption to their development. If you do not feel comfortable initiating physical contact with pupils, then please do not use these particular activities. Your discomfort will be unconsciously read by the child as a sign of threat. Your school may have policy of no touch between staff and pupils, so you may find these activities are not possible. I would recommend asking for a review of this policy, with an emphasis on the benefits of helping children learn the difference between safe and unsafe touch.

As with the group activities the age range given for each activity is only a guide, trust your professional judgement when choosing suitable activities for your pupil. There should be plenty here to get you started and activities can be repeated on more than one occasion, but if you are looking for more ideas, I strongly recommend researching Theraplay, which is focused on strengthening relationships through play. The activities in the Connection Diet have a common objective, context, and time.

Objective: To strengthen the connection between mind and body, and to strengthen the connection with another person.
Context: Connecting with another person and connecting with the self. Strengthening the ventral vagal state through social engagement, body connection and play.
Time: 5-10 minutes.

List of activities for the Connection Diet:

Push Me Over	(age 4-6 years)
What's the Time, Mr Wolf?	(age 4-6 years)
Blow Me Away	(age 4-6 years)
Palm Reading	(age 4-8 years)
Bubbles	(age 4-8 years)
Toilet Paper Burst	(age 4-8 years)
Parachute Tunnels	(age 4-8 years)
Fun with Foil	(age 4-11 years)
Hello, Goodbye	(age 4-11 years)
Balloon Keepy-Uppy	(age 4-11 years)
Punching Newspaper	(age 4-11 years)
Blowing Games	(age 4-11 years)
Mystery Bag	(age 4-11 years)
Movement Stories	(age 4-11 years)
Balancing Games	(age 4-14 years)
Eye Signals	(age 6-11 years)
Rhythm with Cups and Claps	(age 6-14 years)
Squiggle Game	(age 6-18 years)
Making a Rap	(age 8-14 years)
Connecting Card Games	(age 8-18 years)
Standing Mountain	(age 11-18 years)
Seated Forward Fold	(age 11-18 years)
Sun Breaths	(age 11-18 years)

Further Connection Diet activities can be adapted from the group activities given in the previous sections, if pupils have not already done these activities with the group:

Self-Awareness	**Body Maps**	(age 8-18 years)
Connection to the Body	**Clever Toes**	(age 4-18 years)
Connection to the Body	**Sensations Mindfulness**	(age 11-18 years)
Connection to Others	**Handclapping Games**	(age 8-18 years)
Connection to Others	**Mirror-Me**	(age 4-18 years)
Connection to Others	**One-Word Story**	(age 6-18 years)
Self-Soothing	**Sensory Focus**	(age 8-18 years)

Push Me Over

Age range: 4-6 years
Resources: A cushion.
Activity

Kneel or squat so you are at the same height as the child. Hold a cushion between you and the child and both push against it. Challenge the child to try to push you over. Try to stand strong for a little while, then let the child push you over - make it fun by falling down dramatically!

What's the Time, Mr Wolf?

Age range: 4-6 years
Resources: None.
Activity
This is a variation on the traditional game. Instead of standing with your back to the child, face them, from a short distance away. The child asks, 'What's the time, Mr Wolf?' and you reply with a time, such as '3 o'clock!' then the child takes three steps towards you. Continue until the child has almost reached you, then change your answer to 'Cuddle time!' then playfully catch the child and hug them.

Blow Me Away

Age range: 4-6 years.
Resources: None.
Activity
Kneel or squat so you are at the same height as the child. Ask the child to blow at you really hard. Fall over backwards dramatically, as though you have been blown over by a strong wind. Repeat a few times, dramatically trying to resist the strong wind. If the child wants to, you could swap roles.

Palm Reading

Age range: 4-8 years
Resources: Talcum powder or flour.
Activity
Sprinkle the powder or flour on both your hands and the child's hands, then study your hands together to notice shapes and lines. Look for differences and similarities.

Bubbles

Age range: 4-8 years.
Resources: Two small bottles of bubbles with wands.
Activity
Blow bubbles together - you could both try to catch as many bubbles as possible on your wands, or burst them as quickly as you can, or see who can blow the biggest. Make eye-contact with the child as you play. Another variation is that you blow the bubbles, and the child bursts them with a particular part of their body, e.g., their elbows, or feet, or little finger.

Toilet Paper Burst

Age range: 4-8 years.
Resources: A roll of toilet paper.
Activity
Ask the child to stand with their legs together and arms by their side, then wrap their body in toilet paper (not too tight, and not including the neck or head). When they are wrapped up, give them the signal to burst out.

Parachute Tunnels

Age range: 4-8 years.

Resources: A parachute, classroom furniture.

Activity

Using the parachute, create a winding tunnel by supporting it on chairs and desks, etc. The child could help you or you could have it already set up. Ask the child to crawl through the tunnel quickly to either meet you at the end or you could playfully chase them, or you could turn it into a peekaboo game.

Fun with Foil

Age range: 4-11 years

Resources: Aluminium foil and a cushion.

Activity

Lay out a sheet of foil on the cushion and ask the child to push their hand down onto the foil so it makes a print, you may need to help the foil take the shape of their hand. You can try this with their hand in different shapes, e.g., a thumbs up, or with other body parts such as their feet, ear, face, etc. Then study the shapes together.

Hello, Goodbye

Age range: 4-11 years.

Resources: None.

Activity

Explain to the child that this game is called Hello, Goodbye. Start by saying 'hello' to the child in a funny voice and ask if they can say hello in the same funny voice, keep saying hello in various voices, high, low, loud, and quiet, with the child mirroring you. Gauge how comfortable the child is with being dramatic and add gestures and expressions to your 'hellos'. When it is nearly the end of the time you have, switch to saying 'goodbye'. When it is time to finish, ask the child to choose the last way to say goodbye, for you to copy.

Balloon Keepy-Uppy

Age range: 4-11 years.

Resources: A balloon already blown up.

Activity

Throw the balloon up into the air and see how long you can both keep it in the air by hitting it upwards. To make the game harder you could have the rule that you are not allowed to use your hands.

Punching Newspaper

Age range: 4-11 years.

Resources: An old newspaper.

Activity

Kneel or squat so you are at the same height as the child. Hold a sheet of the newspaper stretched out tightly in front of you, at about the child's waist height, for the child to karate chop or punch - make sure they are aiming downwards and not at you. Try with two sheets, then three.

Blowing Games

Age range: 4-11 years.
Resources: Two ping pong balls or cotton balls, two straws.
Activity
Both you and the child have a straw each to blow the balls across the desk or the floor. You could either set up a race or use one ball and have a game of blow-football.

Mystery Bag

Age range: 4-11 years
Resources: A small bag containing mystery items, such as a key, a shell, a marble, a paper-clip, a piece of Lego, a rubber band, a cotton wool ball, etc.
Activity
Ask the child to put their hand in the bag and find an item you name. They aren't allowed to look. Or ask them to find one item and name it before they pull it out of the bag.

Movement Stories

Age range: 4-11 years
Resources: An old bandage, blanket, cushions.
Activity
Explain to the child that you are going to tell them a story that involves them acting out the movements. Make up a short story that involves the following movements: crawling, wrapping up in a blanket, commando-style crawling, jumping, lying down, and rolling over, wrapping up part of the body (e.g., in a bandage). Your story could be a journey involving ideas such as those in Section 5, 'Obstacle Course' activity. The focus is on the movements, not the plot of the story. End the story with something like finding treasure or completing a challenge, so there is a sense of achievement.

Balancing Games

Age range: 4-14 years
Resources: Cushions or soft toys, bean bags.
Activity
Place a cushion or soft toy on the child's head, their challenge is to keep it balanced. You could then add more items, or ask them to walk, or hop while balancing. Another variation is to ask the child to lie on their back with their feet in the air, and you place items on their feet for them to keep balanced.

Eye Signals

Age range: 6–11 years.
Resources: None.
Activity
Explain to the child that you are going to only communicate using eye signals, and your challenge is to move around the room together and get back to the start without any communication other than the eye signals. Hold hands and face each other so you are connected. You could try blinking to indicate the number of steps and look in the direction of travel, etc. Agree the eye signals before setting off because once you start, you can't speak!

Rhythm with Cups and Claps

Age range: 6–14 years.
Resources: Two paper or plastic cups, maybe a device for watching a YouTube video.
Activity
Sit at a desk or table with the child, holding a cup each. By clapping, tapping the cup on the table create a rhythm together. You could start by watching together the clip from the film *Pitch Perfect* where the main character performs a song using a rhythm with tapping a cup and clapping (search 'Pitch Perfect cup song' on YouTube). Copying her would be very ambitious! I would recommend starting off simple.

Squiggle Game

Age range: 6–18 years.
Resources: Two pencils and paper.
Activity
Start with a demonstration. Draw a simple squiggle on a piece of paper, then show the pupil that you can add details to turn the squiggle into something recognisable. Ask the pupil to draw a squiggle, then together decide what it might turn into and together add details to transform the squiggle into a picture.

Making a Rap

Age range: 8–14 years.
Resources: None, maybe a device for watching a YouTube video.
Activity
Choose a topic and create a rap together. You could start by watching the video 'The School Kids Rap' by SchoolKidz TV on YouTube if you are working with a younger child, or for an older child, ask them for a rap you could watch together (making sure the language is appropriate).

Connecting Card Games

Age range: 8–18 years.
Resources: A pack of playing cards, or Uno, or other card game.

Activity

Play any short card game with the young person that is suitable for two people. Pay close attention to the young person, and notice aloud what you observe, for instance, 'I can see that you're smiling, I wonder if you just picked up a good card', 'Wow, you really slammed that card down', 'That's a sneaky look, I wonder what you're going to do next!'. Make sure your observations are not judgemental and try not to state what the pupil is feeling or thinking - 'wondering' works well. The purpose of the observations is for the pupil to feel connected to you through feeling seen by you, and to help them connect with their own actions and expressions, etc.

Standing Mountain

Age range: 11-18 years
Resources: None, maybe a device for watching a YouTube video.
Activity

Do this yoga pose together standing opposite each other, so the pupil's mirror neurones will respond to *you* doing the pose, thereby enhancing the experience for the young person. You could start by watching a video together explaining the pose (search 'standing mountain pose yoga' on YouTube). Focus on bringing attention to the feet and strength in the legs as you stand, then bring your focus to relaxing the shoulders and standing tall. This will help with feeling grounded and confident. Encourage the young person to reflect on why the pose has the name 'standing mountain'.

Seated Forward Fold

Age range: 11-18 years.
Resources: None.
Activity

Sit next to the young person, both facing the same direction, so as you both fold forward you can see each other from the side. Do the fold together, guiding the young person through what you are doing in a slow gentle voice. Make sure your feet are firmly on the floor at about shoulders width apart. Sit tall with relaxed shoulders, like a seated version of the mountain pose. Gently start to lean forwards. You could rest your forearms on your legs so you only fold forward a short way, or you could let your arms hang, so your fingers reach the floor. Notice your breathing and sit back up if it becomes difficult. Frequently check how the young person is feeling - some people might find this position uncomfortable or unsettling, while others might find it calming and comforting. Ask the young person to find a comfortable position in the fold - they might want to gently hold their feet, link their fingers together, hold their elbows with the opposite hands. After a minute or so, ask them to gently lift themselves back up to sitting tall, and notice their breathing.

Sun Breaths

Age range: 11-18 years.
Resources: None.

Activity

This is a good breathing exercise to follow Standing Mountain and/or Seated Forward Fold. Either stand in mountain pose or sit tall, in a seated mountain pose, opposite the young person, so their mirror neurones are activated. Start with your arms outstretched at your side, palms facing upwards, then as you inhale, raise your arms above your head until your palms meet. Hold for a moment, then turn your palms to face downwards as you exhale and lower your arms back to your sides. Talk through the movement and breathing as you do it to start with, then simply repeat, keeping in time with the young person.

Summary

Learning Points

- Group activities are designed to provide a proactive approach to helping pupils develop their capacity for self-regulation. The activities are in sections according to their focus. It is recommended that when planning a programme, activities are chosen from sections in order.
- Group activities are in the sections: 'Warm-ups, Creating a Safe Space – Boundary Setting, Psychoeducation, Self-awareness, Connecting to the Body, Connecting to Others, Self-Soothing'.
- Pupils identified as likely to struggle with the sensitive nature of the activities in a large group should be given a separate programme in a small group with a different member of staff to be delivered at the same time as the main class have their lesson.
- It is recommended that pupils have an exercise book to work in as there are art activities and written exercises.
- It is recommended that time warnings are given towards the ends of activities and lesson to provide a sense of safety for pupils.
- The age range and time for each activity are a guide, use your professional judgement when choosing suitable activities and time planning – you know your class best.
- The final section is the 'Connection Diet' for 1:1 work, not as an alternative to the group activities, but a separate programme for individual pupils who struggle with connecting with themselves and with others. It is recommended as 10 minutes every day at the same time each day.
- It is recommended that you take the PACE attitude to working 1:1 with a child on the Connection Diet, where P = Playfulness, A = Acceptance, C = Curiosity and E = Empathy.
- Mirror neurones are activated in the child when you take an active role in the activity, so it is recommended that you immerse yourself in the activity.

Final Thoughts

Hopefully you now have a sound understanding of **Polyvagal Theory** and how it can be applied in an education setting. We have explored the theory in relation to child development theories and in the context of childhood trauma. We have looked at its application when working with a dysregulated child 'in the moment', as well as its use in proactively promoting the emotional development of all pupils through classroom activities (see Chapter 8 in Part II). There has been an emphasis on *staff* emotional wellbeing being needed for effective support of *pupil* emotional wellbeing, with a chapter dedicated to your own self-care. Finally, an explanation has been given of how a whole school **Polyvagal-informed** approach can be adopted.

I sincerely hope you have found this book helpful. I hope you feel you have better insight into the emotional worlds of your pupils, and their behaviours. I hope you feel better equipped to support children and young people in times of emotional distress, and more empowered to proactively support their social and emotional development.

At the time of writing this book, Polyvagal Theory is fairly unknown in the education profession, so this approach is new to schools. As with any new approach, there needs to be room for criticism, evaluation and improvement, so I welcome any feedback you might have from your experience of implementing the ideas discussed in this book. I am particularly interested in changes you see in your pupils over time, from using the activities in Chapter 8 in Part II of the book, either with classes, or individuals.

As you will have ascertained, I am a firm believer in the application of Polyvagal Theory in improving the emotional wellbeing of ourselves, our colleagues and most of all, the children and young people we work with. Since learning about the theory, I have tried to use my 'Polyvagal lens' in all my interactions, but especially in my work as a child and adolescent therapist, and I have found it something of a game-changer. My hope is to spread the news of this theory and its value to as many education professionals as possible. I truly believe you too will find your new understanding of Polyvagal Theory transformational in the way you work.

DOI: 10.4324/9781003396574-12

Glossary

ACEs (Adverse childhood experiences) distressing, traumatic or abusive experiences before adulthood.

ADHD (Attention Deficit Hyperactivity Disorder) a neurodevelopmental condition that affects a person's behaviour, such as restlessness and difficulties with concentration.

Ambivalent attachment an insecure attachment style caused by the attachment figure seeking closeness to their child in order to meet *their own* needs and therefore not attuning to the needs of the child.

Attachment-aware approach used in schools, this approach to supporting pupils with their behaviours and emotional wellbeing is based on an understanding of attachment theory, and focuses on fostering secure attachments between pupils and staff.

Attachment behaviours a pattern of behaviours towards others developed in infancy and childhood in response to the quality of the attachment with the primary carer.

Attachment style the attachment pattern developed in infancy, of which there are four styles: secure, insecure ambivalent, insecure avoidant and insecure disorganised.

Attachment Theory (Bowlby) the child development theory proposed by John Bowlby that, in order for healthy social and emotional development, a child needs a secure attachment with their primary carer in infancy.

Attunement 'tuning in' to another person's feelings and needs, and responding with understanding and empathy.

Autism known as Autistic Spectrum Disorder (ASD) or Autistic Spectrum Condition (ASC), autism is a neurological and developmental condition that affects how a person acts with others, communicates, learns, and behaves.

Autonomic nervous system (ANS) part of the central nervous system, associated with survival, with the functions of monitoring and regulating essential processes in the body and detecting unconscious cues of threat and cues of safety.

Autonomic states a physiological state (ventral vagal state, sympathetic mobilisation, or dorsal shutdown) brought about by the ANS when it detects cues of safety or cues of threat.

Avoidant attachment an insecure attachment style caused by the attachment figure rejecting the infant, so the infant is caught in an 'approach-avoidance' conflict, as they need contact with their attachment figure for their survival, but this contact involves painful feelings of rejection.

Blended states   the activation of two autonomic states at the same time. Also known as 'dual activation'.

Body tracking   noticing and naming aloud body actions and changes, such as breathing, muscle tension, movement, posture, etc.

Brainstem   one part of the simple triune brain model; the oldest part of the human brain in terms of human evolution, responsible for survival processes. Also called the 'reptilian brain'.

Central nervous system   the system of nerves connecting the body, including the senses, with the brain, enabling two-way communication.

Cognitive Development Theory (Piaget)   the child development theory proposed by Jean Piaget, that involves four stages: Sensorimotor, Preoperational, Concrete Operational and Formal Operational.

Connection Diet   a 1:1 programme of daily 10-minute activities for individual children or young people who have poor connection with their body and with others.

Containment of emotions   the capacity for experiencing strong emotions without being overwhelmed by them, and feeling empathy towards another person who is experiencing strong emotions without becoming overwhelmed by *their* emotions.

Co-regulation   the regulation of emotional intensity with the help of another person, who is themselves self-regulated.

Daily Mile   a health and wellbeing initiative, employed by many schools, in which pupils and staff run, walk or wheel one mile each day together as a group, with the aim of improving physical and emotional wellbeing.

Disorganised attachment   an insecure attachment style caused by the attachment figure responding unpredictably to the infant, being frightening, abusive, and not keeping the infant safe.

Dissociation   a response sometimes found in dorsal shutdown, where the mind can disconnect from the body, the surroundings and even from reality.

Dorsal shutdown state   the autonomic state of feeling under threat and unable to find safety through sympathetic mobilisation; body processes start to shut down.

Dorsal vagal nerve   one of two branches of the vagus nerve, responsible for the dorsal shutdown state.

Dual activation   see *Blended states*.

Dysregulation   the experience of emotional intensity being beyond what is tolerable, causing the person to feel overwhelmed by their emotional state.

EHCP (Education, Health, and Care Plan)   an annually reviewed document that details the educational, health and social care needs of a child or young person, who needs more support than their school can provide, and gives details of the additional support to meet those needs.

ELSA (Emotional Literacy Support Assistant) Intervention   a form of 1:1 support for pupils from a specially trained teaching assistant, focusing on supporting emotional wellbeing with time-limited structured activities.

Empathy   the capacity to understand and share the feelings of another person; happens in the neocortex, therefore requires ventral vagal activation.

Forest School a child-centred holistic learning process, based in nature and facilitated by specially trained staff, supporting play development, social development and supervised risk-taking, to build self-esteem, confidence, resilience, peer relationships and an appreciation of the natural world.

Limbic system one part of the simple triune brain model; the part of the brain above the brainstem predominantly responsible for emotions, attachment, and social behaviour.

Mammalian brain see *Limbic system*.

Maslow's Hierarchy of Needs a model for understanding the needs and motivations of humans from the most basic needs (food, water, sleep, etc.) to most complex needs (morality, creativity, self-fulfilment, etc.).

Mirror neurones neurones in the brain associated with an action, which fire in response to someone else making that action.

Neocortex one part of the simple triune brain model; the youngest part of the brain in terms of human evolution, associated with higher thinking processes, such as language, logic, creativity, and learning

Neuroception a term used for the process by which the autonomic nervous system detects cues of safety and cues of threat, below the level of conscious awareness.

Neurodevelopmental conditions/disorders neurological conditions that affect the development of the brain and nervous system, such as autism, SPD and ADHD.

Neurodivergent a term used to describe a mind that functions significantly differently to what is considered to be typical, including conditions such as ADHD, autism and learning difficulties.

Neuroplasticity the ability of the brain and nervous system to change its function and structure in response to new experience.

PACE (Playfulness, Acceptance, Curiosity, Empathy) an approach, proposed by Dan Hughes, to working with children and young people, based on building safety and trust.

Parasympathetic nervous system part of the ANS, causing a slowing of breathing and heartrate, resulting in the ventral vagal state or dorsal shutdown state; opposite of the sympathetic nervous system.

Polyvagal-informed School a school in which an understanding of Polyvagal Theory is used in supporting pupils with their behaviours and emotional wellbeing.

Polyvagal Theory proposed by Stephen Porges, this theory explains the role of the vagus nerve in emotional regulation, social connection and the body's fear response.

Psychoeducation learning about emotional wellbeing and mental health, including symptoms, causes, common experiences and strategies.

Psychosocial Development Theory (Erikson) the development theory proposed by Erik Erikson focusing on social influences, starting with the development of trust between the infant and their primary carer.

Reptilian brain see *Brainstem*.

Resilience the capacity to tolerate difficult feelings and cope in challenging situations.

Secure attachment the attachment style developed where the attachment figure responds to the infant with sensitivity, understanding and empathy, and the needs of the infant are met.

Secure base the relationship an infant develops with their primary carer (usually their mother) where their physical and emotional needs are met with effective attunement.

Self-regulation the capacity for a person to regulate their own emotional intensity without help from another person.

Social engagement system a system within the neocortex for connecting with other people, that has a strong connection with the ventral vagal state.

Sociocultural Theory (Vygotsky) the child development theory proposed by Lev Vygotsky, emphasising social influence on cognitive development.

Somatisation a physical experience as a response to strong emotions, e.g., headache caused by anxiety.

SPD (Sensory Processing Disorder) a condition that affects how the brain processes sensory information, i.e., input from sight, hearing, smell, taste and touch. SPD can affect any or all of the senses.

Sympathetic mobilisation state the autonomic state of feeling under threat, and responding with 'fight, flight or freeze'; body processes adapted for mobilisation.

Sympathetic nervous system part of the ANS that causes physiological mobilisation, such as speeding up of breathing and heartrate, resulting in the sympathetic mobilisation state; opposite of the parasympathetic nervous system.

Thrive approach used by schools, this intervention to meet the emotional and social needs of pupils is facilitated by a Thrive-trained practitioner, and is trauma-sensitive, time-limited and structured.

Trauma an experience beyond the range of normal human life experiences, that causes significant distress.

Trauma-informed approach used in schools, this approach to supporting pupils with their behaviours and emotional wellbeing is based on an understanding of the effects of trauma on the individual.

Triune brain a simple three-part model for understanding the human brain, comprising of the brainstem, the limbic system, and the neocortex.

Vagal brake the function of the ventral vagal nerve which slows down or speeds up the heartrate. A healthy vagal brake allows easy transition between autonomic states, as the heartrate is easily regulated.

Vagus nerve the nerve connecting the brain to the body in the parasympathetic nervous system, with two branches: the ventral vagal nerve and dorsal vagal nerve.

Ventral vagal nerve one of two branches of the vagus nerve, responsible for the ventral vagal state.

Ventral vagal net a model for visualising a staff *group* ventral vagal state, where staff members are the junctions, connected to each other through supportive relationships.

Ventral vagal state the autonomic state of feeling safe, calm, and grounded; body processes at their most efficient.

Zones of Regulation used in school, this approach focuses on developing the pupil's capacity to self-regulate through self-awareness and use of self-soothing strategies.

References

APA (American Psychiatric Association) (2013) *Diagnostic and Statistical Manual of Mental Disorders: DSM-5*, 5th edn. Washington, DC: American Psychiatric Publishing.

Badenoch, B. (2008) *Being a Brain-wise Therapist: A Practical Guide to Interpersonal Neurobiology*, New York: W. W. Norton & Company.

Bowlby, J. (1969) *Attachment and Loss*, vol. 1, London: Pimlico.

Dana, D. (2020) *Polyvagal Exercises for Safety and Connection: 50 Client-centered Practices*, New York: W. W. Norton & Company.

Department for Education (2023) *Keeping Children safe in Education 2023: Statutory Guidance for Schools and Colleges*. Available at www.gov.uk (accessed 18th February 2024).

Dion, L. (2018) *Aggression in Play Therapy: A Neurological Approach for Integrating Intensity*, New York: W. W. Norton & Company.

Dispenza, J. (2007) *Evolve Your Brain: The Science of Changing Your Mind*, Deerfield Beach, FL: Health Communications.

Dr Seuss (1996) *My Many Coloured Days*, London: Random House Children's Publishers UK.

Emerson, D. and Hopper, E. (2011) *Overcoming Trauma through Yoga: Reclaiming Your Body*, Berkeley, CA: North Atlantic Books.

Erikson, E.H. and Erikson, J.M. (1997) *The Life Cycle Completed: Extended Version*, New York: W. W. Norton & Company.

Fontana, D. and Slack, I. (1997) *Teaching Meditation to Children*, Shaftsbury, Dorset: Element Books.

Ford, K., Quigg, Z., Hughes, K. et al. (2016) Understanding the Impact of Adverse Childhood Experiences on Health and Wellbeing in England, *Injury Prevention* 22: A104.

Gascoyne, S. (2019) *Messy Play in the Early Years: Supporting Learning through Materials Engagement*, Abingdon: Routledge.

Geddes, H. (2006) *Attachment in the Classroom: The Links between Children's Early Experience, Emotional Well-being and Performance in School*, London: Worth Publishing.

Gerhardt, S. (2015) *Why Love Matters: How Affection Shapes a Baby's Brain*, Hove: Routledge.

Hughes, D., Phillips, S. and Melim, D. (2020) *Belonging: A Relationship-based Approach for Trauma-informed Education*, Lanham, MD: Rowman & Littlefield.

Levine, P. (1997) *Waking the Tiger: Healing Trauma*, Berkeley, CA: North Atlantic Books.

Lloyd, S. (2016) *Improving Sensory Processing in Traumatized Children*, London: Jessica Kingsley Publishers.

Mosley, J. (1996) *Quality Circle Time in the Primary Classroom*, Cambs: LDA.

Newlove-Delgado, T., Marcheselli, F., Williams, T., Mandalia, D.. Davis, J., McManus, S., Savic, M., Treloar, W. and Ford, T. (2022) *Mental Health of Children and Young People in England*, Leeds: NHS Digital.

NHS (2022) Causes – Post-Traumatic Stress Disorder. Available at: www.nhs.uk (accessed 4 February 2023).

Norris, V. and Rodwell, H. (2017) *Parenting with Theraplay*, London: Jessica Kingsley Publishers.

Piaget, J. and Inhelder, B. (1969) *The Psychology of the Child*, New York: Basic Books.

Porges, S.W. (2003) The Polyvagal Theory: Phylogenetic Contributions to Social behaviour, *Physiology and Behaviour* 79(3): 503–513.

Porges, S.W. (2009) The Polyvagal Theory: New Insights into Adaptive Reactions of the Autonomic Nervous System, *Cleveland Clinic Journal of Medicine* 76: S86–S90.

Porges, S.W. (2017) *The Pocket Guide to Polyvagal Theory: The Transformative Power of Feeling Safe*, New York: W. W. Norton & Company.

Portis, A. (2009) *Not a Stick*, New York: HarperCollins Publishers.

Puddicombe, A. (2011) *Get Some Headspace: 10 Minutes Can Make All the Difference*, London: Hodder & Stoughton.

Sanders, M. and Thompson, G. (2022) *Polyvagal Theory and the Developing Child*, New York: W. W. Norton & Company.

Santrock, J. W. (2001) *Child Development*, New York: McGraw-Hill Higher Education.

Van Der Kolk, B. (2014) *The Body Keeps the Score: Mind, Brain and Body in the Transformation of Trauma*, London: Penguin Books.

Viner. R. et al. (2022) Impacts of School Closures on Physical and Mental Health of Children and Young People: A Systematic Review, *JAMA Pediatrics* 176(4): 400–409.

Winnicott, D. W. (1964) *The Child, the Family and the Outside World*, London: Penguin Books.

World Health Organization (2019/2021) *International Classification of Diseases*, Eleventh Revision (ICD-11), Geneva: World Health Organization (WHO).

Index

For Product Safety Concerns and Information please contact our EU
representative GPSR@taylorandfrancis.com Taylor & Francis Verlag GmbH,
Kaufingerstraße 24, 80331 München, Germany

Printed and bound by CPI Group (UK) Ltd, Croydon, CR0 4YY
08/06/2025
01897000-0020